"Great recruiting advice. 1
information that a player c
coaches."

> Tom Fleenor
> Recruiting Coordinator, USC Spartanburg
> Spartanburg, S.C.

"The college search process for a parent of a baseball player is an
incredible ordeal. I wish this book had been around when we
started the process for my older son. I'll definitely make use of it
when my younger son heads down that (base) path. Peak Power
Baseball offers great information not easily found elsewhere for any
high school player aspiring to play ball in college."

> Paul J. Neal, Jr., Esq.
> Ten Year Youth League Coach
> Seven Year Local Little League President

"For the high school baseball player, Peak Power Baseball will be
a much used resource in their quest to reach great heights in the
great game of baseball. For the high school coach to the athlete's
parents, this book will become invaluable in the various aspects of
the total education of a player on and off the diamond."

> Bill Dod
> Athletic Director - Varsity Baseball Coach
> Souhegan High School, Amherst, NH

"You don't need a big body to play major league baseball - just a
big heart. Peak Power Baseball's chapter on David Eckstein points
this out quite nicely."

> Johnny Pesky
> Special Assistant Player Development
> Boston Red Sox

PEAK *POWER* BASEBALL

How To Turn Your
Little League Dream
Into Major League Reality

Power Publications, Inc.

Longwood, FL 32750

Disclaimer: This book is intended as a reference volume only. The information contained within is intended to help you make informed decisions about your diet and exercise, and not to substitute for any treatment that may have been prescribed by your physician. Keep in mind that nutritional and exercise needs vary from person to person. Anyone considering an exercise or supplement program should obtain approval from his health care provider before beginning such a program. Because there may be some individual risk involved, the publisher and contributing authors are not responsible for any adverse effects or consequences resulting from the use or misuse of any of the suggestions, information, exercises or other content in this book. The information provided is simply designed to be an educational resource to guide you on your personal quest toward a baseball career.

Acknowledgements

Baseball has been a big part of my family's life over the years, and I want to acknowledge and thank all of those who have helped make this, for me, the greatest game in the world.

My father, Harold Vigue, introduced me to baseball. He was part of a State Championship American Legion Team in Maine in 1939, and he taught me the game he loved so much.

My brother, John Vigue, was part of a State Championship Little League team in Maine in the 1960's. He was MVP of his high school team, and we spent hour after hour tossing the ball back and forth.

A real influence for me in baseball was all the guys who played at Skumway field: Bobby and Ricky Boucher, Danny (Sam) and Bobby Cosgrove, Dave and Bruce Willette, Paul Pooler, and Monty the Cat Smith. We had great times playing opposite-side-home-run-derby.

During my coaching years, I had the privilege of working with the greatest Little League Director in the country, Fran Purnell, as well as coaches' Jeff Gardiner, Bruce Kingdon, Nate Stubbert, Dick and George Whitten, Alan Tuttle and Rod Fergerson.

I grew up on the same street that John Winkin lived on. John is truly one of the great college coaches in the history of the sport and a true inspiration. Now in his 80's, he is still contributing by coaching, writing a regular column in *Collegiate Baseball* magazine, and writing great instructional books for coaches and players alike.

Finally, I'd like to thank my mother, Evangeline (Van) Vigue, who was the world's greatest fan; and my son, Kris, who is the best player ever from our family. Even if he were never to play another game, I am very proud of what he has accomplished in baseball. He also was recently part of a State Championship American Legion team in Florida in 2002, which adds another generation of championships to the family.

It is my hope that this book will give back to baseball a little bit of what baseball has given to my family and me over the years.

Table of Contents

Foreword

by Chipper Jones

Like a lot of kids in America I grew up living, breathing, and talking baseball. My dad, who at the time was a high school teacher and baseball coach, played baseball through college and the minor league ranks. It just seemed natural for me to have a baseball and bat in my hands from the time I could walk. I would go to the field with my dad, and all the high school kids would play catch with me and pitch to me as I swung a bat that felt like a huge metal pole in my hands. While I played all sports growing up, I knew from a very young age that baseball was going to be the place where I had a chance to succeed at the highest levels. It was where my passion lay, and the baseball field was where I knew I belonged.

While I was growing up in Pierson, Florida, I was surrounded by hard working folks who had made farming their lives. From Little League to Babe Ruth to American Legion, I was constantly being pushed to be a better player by the older kids who were on my teams. It was never easy, and while I was younger it was very difficult at times, but it always pushed me to be the type of player that I wanted to be. *Peak Power Baseball* is all about pushing you to be the type of player that you want to be.

One day after my freshman year of high school my parents decided that it was time to push me again in the direction of becoming a better person and baseball player. My life would never be the same. On that day, my parents enrolled me at the Bolles School, a boarding school in Jacksonville, Florida, and 1 1/2 hours from my hometown. It was extremely difficult at first as I was homesick, missed my friends, and was experiencing academic challenges that I had not yet faced. Obviously, it was tough on my parents, too, but they knew that I needed to be challenged in several aspects of my life. Over the next few years, I realized that being sent to Bolles was the best thing that had ever happened to me. While I was certainly successful in my hometown and did well in classes there, I was an unknown at Bolles. I was placed in a position of having to prove myself all over again. No player, coach or teacher knew who Chipper Jones was when I arrived at Bolles on the first day of classes. This fact was extremely important, because it pushed me to prove myself all over again on the field and in the classroom.

On the field, my life was dedicated to becoming a major league baseball player. If I was not in the cage hitting, I was on the field taking fungoes and throwing across the diamond. Although weight training is now a big part of my regimen, I did not lift much when I was younger. I was completely tuned into making myself better on the field. I worked to become as fundamentally sound as possible. I would sometimes hit until blisters stopped me in my tracks. I would take ground balls until my legs, arms and feet couldn't bear to take one more. To me, it was about being the best baseball player I could be. Nothing was going to stop me.

In June 1990, the Atlanta Braves selected me with the first pick of the 1990 Amateur Draft. At that moment, all of my hard work and commitment had paid off. It wasn't so much that I was the first pick of the draft. It was that I was finally going to get the opportunity to play professional baseball. I had studied hard and received a scholarship offer to attend the University of Miami, and was intent on going there if the draft didn't work out for me. Getting the job done in the classroom allowed me to be in the win-win position I was then in. With all of this on my side, when the Braves called me on that day in June, I knew that I had really arrived.

The years that followed brought me many ups and downs in the Braves' minor league system, but it also brought me a World Series Championship in 1995, and a National League MVP Award in 1999. But, it was on those fields in Pierson and Jacksonville where I truly made all of these dreams come true. Many people think that major league ballplayers are born with the talent that gets them to the big leagues. While I was certainly blessed with good genes, God given talent, and some good luck, I put in hours and hours of hard work to turn myself into the kind of ballplayer that I wanted to be. The great thing about baseball is that you have to work at it constantly to maintain a level of consistently. While I loved doing it, I played in hundreds of games and put in thousands of hours of practice. Throughout my high school career and continuing today, I put in the work I feel is necessary to be successful. I take thousands of cuts each off-season. During spring training, I am constantly taking fungoes or fly balls. Even during the year, I watch video and take extra batting practice when I am having problems at the plate. Unfortunately, people only see me on the field during games. I think the perception is that I simply show up at game time, go out there, and just start playing. The things they don't see is me working out five times a week in the weight room doing a series of powerful core training exercises, or me hitting for an hour a day in a cage that I built on my ranch, or the countless hours during the season spent watching tape, and hitting in the cage at the field when things are going badly.

As a baseball player, and an athlete in general, I take pride in my job. I realize that I am expected to perform at a very high level; but those expectations are dwarfed by the level of expectations that I have for myself. It is this expectation that drives me to work as hard as I do on and off the field.

A book like *Peak Power Baseball* would have definitely helped me in this long process, and I wish it had been around when I started out. There is a wealth of information in this book to which every ballplayer that has the ambition to play college or professional baseball can relate. Everything from nutrition to weight training to baseball drills is addressed in this comprehensive book. While I know that everyone that reads this book will not be a major league or college player, it will certainly help you become the best player that you are capable of becoming. Many youngsters have asked me what they need to do to make it to the big leagues. The answer: out-work every other person on the field, and understand the importance of hard work and education. Then no matter what happens with your career, you will be a better person for it. Work hard, play hard, and maybe someday I'll see you in the bigs.

Take care and good luck.

Chipper Jones

Introduction

by Patrick J. Cohn, Ph.D.

Unless an athlete has more physical talent than his peers, he is forced to adopt a multi-dimensional training approach to keep up with the competition. That's why more players are engaging in sports-specific training, working with hitting coaches, seeking nutritional guidance, and working with sport psychologists. *Peak Power Baseball* is a comprehensive guide and preparation program for serious players who want to play collegiate or professional baseball.

This total training program draws expertise from several authorities in their respective disciplines to help you train better, learn faster, and thus perform better. In these pages you'll learn the latest methods to help you reach your peak performance. Experts in the fields of baseball strategy, scouting, hitting instruction, baseball psychology, coaching, strength and conditioning, sports vision, slump-busting, marketing, and nutrition share their choice strategies. These experts present a complete baseball-specific program by integrating the disciplines that are vital in order to stay competitive and to get the edge over your competitors.

PGA Tour star Tiger Woods is a good example of the effects of a comprehensive training program including swing mechanics, sport psychology, physical therapy, and exercise science to become a dominant player in the sport of golf. With the guidance of his father Tiger Woods trained and prepared for every facet of his game from an early age. He worked with a PGA instructor, sports psychologist, athletic trainer, physical therapist, and equipment specialist.

Sports are becoming more and more competitive today. Baseball players are bigger, stronger, mentally tougher, and better trained. To stay competitive, an athlete must keep up with the advances made in peak performance enhancement by engaging in several types of training programs, including sport-specific training and practice regimens. If you are not taking advantage of advances in baseball instruction, sports psychology, physical therapy, nutrition, and exercise science, your competitors will pass you by.

The game of baseball presents unique demands and is one of the most challenging games you can play. The mental, physical, and strategic challenges of the game make baseball both fun and frustrating. You can only go so far with raw physical talent. To reach your potential, talent must be refined and polished. The best players in baseball (Chipper Jones, Sammy Sosa, and Barry Bonds, to name a few) have tremendous talent, but they have combined their abilities with hard work, hours of practice, and mental discipline. They prepare to win. These great players know how to train, practice, and prepare to get the most out of their physical ability. Players have a lot of information to choose from on the proper swing mechanics, equipment, strategy, and mental game. The challenge is to decide which expert you should listen to. Like other sports, baseball is filled with differing philosophies about how to play, teach, or become great. The challenge is to unscramble all the information and uncover what's right for you. *Peak Power Baseball* brings together the sources to help you do just this: to achieve your goals in baseball – and beyond.

To perform at peak performance levels, players today must stay physically healthy, avoid injury, have sound mechanics, be mentally tough, eat right, and practice efficiently. You may improve by figuring this all out on your own, but I believe you can achieve greater results, without spending more time than you do now, by utilizing the expertise of the authorities in *Peak Power Baseball*. It is a book that goes beyond helping you to become a complete player by giving you an inside look at what scouts and coaches look for in a ballplayer, and the pros and cons of playing college or professional baseball out of high school.

You may have superior talent to play baseball, but talent alone will only get you so far. You need the complete package to compete. Proper instruction, a sports-specific fitness program, and mental game skills are all necessary to reach your peak. In addition, motivation, desire, and commitment are the foundations of a champion ball player.

Great athletes use every available performance enhancement tool available to help them succeed. This book combines many sources in sports science and coaching to help you get the mental, strategic, and physical advantage. You can begin by tapping the resources of this book, yet no real learning has occurred until you apply what you learn on the baseball field. I always tell my students that learning is a three-part process. First, you gain the information that can potentially make you a better player. Second, you apply what you learn to your training, practice routines, and play. Third, you have to commit to striving for excellence each day, week, and month – in and out of the baseball season. Only with a commitment to your goals and training program can you fully realize your potential as an athlete. Helping you achieve that is the goal of *Peak Power Baseball.*

Patrick J. Cohn, Ph.D.

Dr. Patrick J. Cohn heads *Peak Performance Sports* in Orlando, Florida. A leading sports and golf psychologist, author, and professional speaker, Dr. Cohn teaches sports psychology to amateur, professional, and collegiate athletes. He is the author of *The Mental Game of Golf, Peak Performance Golf, Going Low,* and *The Mental Art of Putting.* For more information on one-on-one mental game coaching or team seminars, visit Peak Performance Sports' web-site at *www.peaksports.com.* To contact Dr. Cohn, e-mail him at *doccohn@aol.com* or call 888-742-7225.

CHAPTER 1

What College Coaches Look For And What Athletes Can Expect From A College

Tom Riginos
Former Head Recruiter
Stetson University, Florida

What do college coaches look for in a player? How do they find and recruit top talent?

First of all, I should point out that all coaches are different. Different coaches with different philosophies look for different attributes in players. I always tell people the old adage, "That beauty is in the eye of the beholder." What I look for may be totally different than what someone else might look for.

I want first and foremost to see players play the game. Receiving statistics or showcase results in the mail from a player might tell me how fast someone runs or what his throwing velocity is, but it doesn't tell me much about how the player plays the game. I look for someone who has a feel for the game of baseball. I watch for little things, such as: Does he hustle all-out after hitting a ground ball to short? Does he back-up throws? Does he know where he is supposed to be on the field at all times? Is he a team leader? Does he understand how the game is supposed to be played? I can't see these things by simply looking at statistics. I need to see a player in actual game situations.

I also look for intelligent ballplayers. Players need to understand a college team's philosophy and be smart enough to execute its game plan. A basic intelligence and understanding of how baseball is played is very important. As a former Assistant Coach for Stetson University, I also know that players need that intelligence to be able to handle their college academics.

The second thing I look for is raw physical ability. Can a player run and hit? Can he play defense?

♦ For outfielders I need to know what kind of arms they have and if they have good foot-speed to get to a ball. I don't pay that much attention to raw numbers, but I'd say an outfielder would have to run at least a 7-flat-or-better 60-yard dash to play for a good Division I program. Of course, if the athlete is an outstanding hitter, that could compensate for being a slower runner.

♦ For infielders I look for athletic players with excellent range and strong defensive abilities. Again, they definitely have to have a basic intelligence, especially at shortstop, which I consider the captain of the field.

♦ Catchers need to be very strong defensively with strong throwing arms. They need to have strong bodies that will endure the rigors of competitive Division I baseball. If a catcher is strong defensively, it is always a plus to have him be strong offensively; but he can play even if he isn't.

♦ With pitchers I would like to see at least two pitches that can be thrown for strikes. I would prefer to see three, but two is definitely mandatory. Velocity isn't everything. A pitcher doesn't have to throw 90 MPH to pitch for a good Division I program. If he does, that's great, but if someone is throwing 84-86 MPH with good movement on his fastball, he can probably pitch. I like to see a pitcher's curve ball thrown consistently for strikes, and I would like to see a good change-up that can be thrown anytime in the count.

As for size I am not hung up on the prototypical 6'3" – 200-lb. pitcher's body type. Some coaches want to see size in a pitcher, but I'm not that concerned. If a player is 5'9" and 170 lbs. and can throw the pitches I mentioned above with consistency and has decent velocity and ball movement, I'll recruit him just as I would if he were 6'3".

Again, I am not real concerned with body types. As an example, in 2001, Stetson University had two 5'9" players that signed professional contracts, and each hit over 16 home runs. If you are a good ballplayer, size should not matter.

One question I'm usually asked is how do colleges find the majority of their recruits? The answer is, in many ways. Stetson gets potential recruits from high school coaches, pro scouts, alumni, former players, showcases, tournaments, and recruiting services. They take all of these into consideration, but the best method for them, however, is to have their coaches actually get out and see games. They get names in lots of ways, but the players they actually recruit are the ones they actually see, and they see most of their prospects in the summer.

On average Stetson receives 1,000 to 1,500 inquiries per year. Their policy is to send out a letter and prospect card to all of them. They do this regardless of how they are contacted, whether it is by e-mail, letter or a call. With this many players it is almost impossible to follow up on each and every one of them. If they have a good relationship with a coach, they will probably follow up. If something jumps out of a letter (for example, the player throws 92 MPH or runs the sixty-yard dash in 6.4), they will follow up. But for the rest they basically go into a database. When a coach visits other parts of the country, he will see who has written them from that area and follow up when there. Of course, if someone makes his information really stand out, (like a good resume) they would probably be more inclined to seek that player out. Of the 1,000-1,500 players a year who initially get in touch with Stetson, they probably call 100-120. It is with these players they seek more information and see where Stetson stands on their list of colleges.

Unless I actually see a player, it is very difficult for me to recruit him. While at Stetson we had one ballplayer from out-of-state who began sending us letters in February of his junior year. He continued to send us letter after letter with statistics, awards, coach's recommendations, and other items of interest. His family moved to Florida and he continued to send us information such as showcase results. We invited him to our hitting camp, and when we actually saw him hit over a couple day period, we were impressed enough to offer him a spot on the team. Here's a player who had some abilities and did everything he could to get our attention, but probably would have slipped through the cracks until we had a chance to see him in action.

If a player doesn't believe that the coach of the college of his choice will get an opportunity to see him, I highly recommend attending that school's baseball camp. I understand that out-of-state players can't be traveling to several camps at schools they are interested in, but if you truly believe you have what it takes to play for a particular program, I would strongly advise you to make the effort and attend that school's camp. While you are there have the coaches of that school critique your skill level. They'll tell you if you have what it takes to play for their program. The earlier you get started the better.

Today players wait until their senior year to start marketing themselves. That's often too late. Begin early (even your sophomore year isn't too early). You definitely should be getting your name out as a junior and attending showcases and camps.

NCAA Division I schools are allotted 11.7 scholarships which are usually broken up by percentage. At Stetson they usually carry between 30 and 32 players. As you can see they can't give all of them a full scholarship. The fact is in baseball there are very few full scholarships. Junior colleges have more scholarships to offer, and that's why a lot of good players end up going to a junior college for a couple of years. You can also be drafted after every year of junior college, but a Division I player has to wait until after his junior year to sign. Because Stetson is expensive compared to state universities, they hope that their players will also get some academic money. If they recruit academically strong players (3.5 GPA, 1200 SAT, or is in the top 10% of his class), the player's academic scholarship won't count toward their 11.7 baseball scholarships. So you can see, it is important for them to get good students as well as good ballplayers.

Of the 1,000-1,500 players that initially get in touch with Stetson, they begin calling approximately 120 of them. After their initial calls, the list is cut down further. Either the player isn't interested in Stetson, or Stetson isn't interested in them. By August they might have the list down to 35 names. They are allowed a maximum of twenty-five official visits. Depending on the specific needs of the team in any one year, they may offer official visits to 10-15 players. A player can have five official visits, and the coaches want Stetson to be in a player's top three before they will offer him an official visit.

Since scholarships are limited, they may make three kids an offer, and whoever takes it first, gets it. Once a player signs and comes to Stetson, they will do everything they can to make him successful in classes and on the ball field.

Players can walk on, but there is a difference between a recruited walk-on and an uninvited walk-on. A recruited walk-on is a player who has a good chance of making the team but doesn't have any athletic scholarship. At Stetson, 100% of their recruited walk-ons will make the team and have the opportunity of earning baseball scholarship monies down the road based on performance. In a school their size they have only a few uninvited walk-ons, and the number actually making the team is very small – maybe one a year, if that.

Division I baseball is a big commitment and not every player can handle it. The actual practice time is limited to 20 hours per week by the NCAA, but players can also practice on their own without a coach being present. At Stetson practices usually run during the week from 2:45 P.M. to 5:45 P.M., and there is usually a four-hour practice on Saturdays when they don't have a game. At a school like Stetson, you can figure an average of 2 ½ - 3 hours of schoolwork per night, so you can quickly see that a player needs to budget his time wisely.

Stetson also has a mandatory study hall three times a week for two hours. The school has tutors available and an academic coordinator on staff. The coordinator offers a study skills program that goes over note-taking, reading strategies and test taking, and provides the coaches with progress reports so they always know how their players are doing. When you combine this with Stetson's 11-1 student-teacher ratio, their players aren't just numbers. They do whatever it takes to make sure their players are successful on and off the field.

There are several things a player looks for when choosing a school, and realistically they will find several pluses and minuses with each college they look at. Again, using Stetson as an example, their negatives are few, but they do have them. They are fairly expensive, they don't have a football team, they are a small school (2,100 students), and they aren't located in a big city, although they aren't that far away from one (Orlando). They also, however, have several pluses. They are in Florida and within driving distance of great beaches and great entertainment. They are well respected academically: 95% of their professors have their Ph.D. They also have a unique program where good students can do their undergraduate work in three years and gain automatic entrance to their nationally respected law school in St. Petersburg. They also have a very strong baseball tradition and outstanding facilities, and they play in a very competitive conference. Their coaching staff is committed to the program and *U.S. News and World Report* consistently rates them in the top five of regional universities.

In summary, a coach has to find a player that is right for their program, and a player has to find a school that meets his needs. When the two come together, it can become a very successful relationship.

Tom Riginos

Former Recruiting Coordinator and
Assistant Baseball Coach
Stetson University, Deland, Florida

As former recruiting coordinator and assistant baseball coach for Florida's Stetson University of Deland, Florida, nationally recognized Tom Riginos was always looking for baseball talent. A graduate of Stetson himself (with a B.A. in Sports Administration in 1990), Tom played centerfield under Head Coach, Pete Dunn.

In 1993 he received his Masters Degree in Sports Administration from Eastern Kentucky University, where he served as assistant coach for two years. Also in 1993, he was offered a position as second coaching assistant at Stetson University, a position he held for four years before accepting the position of assistant baseball coach and recruiting coordinator. Tom specializes in working with outfielders and hitters. This is in addition to his recruiting responsibilities. Tom's expertise, however, is shown by the type of player he recruits. *Collegiate Baseball* has recognized Tom's last seven recruiting classes, and since 1995, Stetson has had eleven freshman All-Americans, proving that he and Stetson's program are not afraid to utilize talented freshmen in the lineup.

Stetson has had four conference championships since 1988, and has been to the NCAA Regional Tournament eleven times. A perennial top-thirty team, Stetson is usually the smallest school in the national rankings.

In 2002, Tom left Stetson to take the position of assistant baseball coach for Clemson University in South Carolina.

On November 22, 2000, Tom and his wife, Shaileen, welcomed the birth of their twin daughters, Alexandra and Grace.

Tom can be reached at: Tom Riginos, Clemson Baseball, Jervey Athletic Center, PO Box 31, Clemson, SC 29633, Phone 864-656-1950, or e-mail at Trigino@Clemson.edu.

To reach Stetson University contact Assistant Coach Terry Rooney, Phone: 386-822-8122; e-mail at Trooney@stetson.edu.

CHAPTER 2

What Is The Right College For You?

Joe Barth, Jr.
The Hit Doctor®

I firmly believe that there is a college for every good high school player. National statistics tell us that only one out of every ten high school ballplayers ends up playing college ball, but I believe that all capable ballplayers should be able to play ball in college somewhere.

One of the biggest problems I see for players is that they wait until the last minute to try and find a school. I believe that players need to get their names out there with letters, e-mails, and by attending camps and showcases as early as the sophomore year. Parents need to take an active role in helping their child do this because by a player's junior year, he should already have a few prospective schools interested in him.

When I say showcases, I don't mean ones in your own backyard. It makes little sense to attend a local showcase because most coaches from your area already know you. National showcases are good because they open doors to other areas, but no showcase can hurt a player, and can often help.

At our showcases we rate our players on a national high school scale. This lets a player find out where he is realistically capable of playing. If he is a Division I caliber player, our rating system will help point that out. If he is a Division III player, that will show up as well. We are not infallible, but we have a good track record, and coaches trust our assessments.

If you look at the player evaluation form at the end of this chapter, it will give you an idea of how we rate players. For instance, if an infielder throws across the diamond at 86-87 MPH, he will get a 10 rating from us. If you look at the *general national player rating scale*, it shows a 9-10 as a pro prospect rating. Let's say this same infielder runs a 7.35 60-yard dash. His rating here would only be a 5, which is an above-average to a well-above-average high school player. We will grade hitting, power and fielding, as well as come up with an overall present rating and an overall projected rating. Someone could be a well-above-average high school player now, but be a projected pro prospect in the future.

We attempt to evaluate a player's baseball tools as honestly as we can based on his performance at our showcase. We rate players on a national scale, so a player getting a 6 rating in Florida is comparable to a 6 rating in California. Our ratings are mostly based on objective scales, which we use for all players at all sites. Very little of our evaluation is subjective.

As I mentioned before, a player's overall rating includes both a present and a projected number. The projected number represents the level we think a player is capable of achieving based on varying factors. The factors may include: a player's age (we assume a younger player will continue to develop); a player's physical build (example: a tall, slim pitcher can increase velocity by filling out, gaining weight, strength training); a player's mechanics (poor mechanics can be corrected).

Each player receives a printed evaluation of his performance, appropriate for photocopying and sending to coaches as a reference. We also mail the player reports from all sites to colleges all over the country and e-mail a link to reports posted on our web-site to every college coach in the country with a published e-mail address. Players may request that their results be withheld from these reports if they wish. I have schools at every level that believe in our assessments and act on them. Even if a player gets what he considers a low number, there will be schools that contact him, because every school needs players, but each needs players at different playing levels. Some schools have specific needs, but I firmly believe that there are places for every decent player to go, and good players for every college.

If a player is good and comes from a warm weather state, there usually is a place for him to play. If a player comes from a cold weather state, he has to work a little harder. Most of our players, however, are playing somewhere regardless of where they are from. A lot of them said it was because their names were sent to some little known colleges, and they received letters from them. We are getting a lot of players placed, but it might be at a school in the Mid-Atlantic region or the West. Big schools in Florida usually don't recruit outside of Florida unless the prospect is a total stud. Most Northern kids end up in the Mid-Atlantic area – Virginia for instance. It is very difficult for a northern kid to crack a Florida school.

A lot of good players from Texas, California and Florida who didn't get drafted or weren't ready for Division I ball for one reason or another end up going to a junior college for a year or two. If they perform well, they hope to eventually get drafted or recruited by a Division I school. Junior college ball in Southern states is often very competitive.

If a player is in the top 100 or 200 high school players in the country, he probably doesn't need a program such as ours. Our program really caters to undiscovered upperclassmen. They may be Division I prospects, but because of where they play or where they live, no one knows about them. We have had kids who were total studs get a 9 or a 10 rating at our camp and no one had ever heard about them before. That is not the norm lately, however, because coaches and recruiters talk and know the players, but we still get one or two a year.

We want to help all players get into a good college baseball program, and as a result, also focus on the Division II or NAIA players to help them get placed. We give underclassmen a reality check as to where their skill level will allow them to play. We show them where they are in comparison to other players already playing college ball. They may think they are a Division I player, but we show them realistically where their skills will allow them to play. But we don't stop there; we also give them the information they need to improve if they aren't happy with their assessment. We can tell them what they need to do to get to the colleges they want to get to.

Once we get a player's name out there, he needs to be prepared to hear from various programs. A player should also be aware of NCAA regulations. Since 1993 all players who wish to participate in any NCAA Division I or Division II programs must submit an application to the *NCAA Clearinghouse* and receive a letter of eligibility. Some high school guidance counselors are not yet familiar with these rules and guidelines, so it is up to the player to be responsible for his own eligibility status and to take appropriate steps to secure it. This requirement also applies to home-schooled student athletes. It has been our experience that many players are not even aware of the existence of the Clearinghouse. To get information, you should check out the NCAA web-site at or call the NCAA hotline at 1-800-638-3731.

I should also point out that when we mail a list of appropriate schools to a player for a player's rating, this is based strictly on physical skills. We do not take into account the academic requirements of any particular school.

All colleges have a minimum requirement with regards to overall grade point average (GPA) and SAT or ACT scores in order for a student to be admitted. However, some schools will lower the requirement for a student athlete depending on the desire of the coach to have that athlete admitted. Other schools simply go by minimums no matter how good the athlete is. For example, if you don't get a minimum 500 on your SAT verbal, they simply won't admit you. However, no athlete can play at any NCAA Division I or Division II program without the minimum GPA and SAT requirements of the *NCAA Clearinghouse*. These requirements often change and may be different at different NCAA Division Levels. A player needs to know what the current minimums are. Also an overall grade point average is different from the Clearinghouse's grade point average. The

Clearinghouse calculates the GPA from thirteen core curriculum courses, which are clearly named. These thirteen core courses include a certain number of English, Math, Science and History courses, with an addition of some approved electives. The course curriculum has been pre-approved by the Clearinghouse, and all high school players are required to complete it. In thirteen of these particular NCAA Clearinghouse approved courses, you must have the minimum grade point average. If your overall GPA is borderline, it may have been boosted by electives, which are not approved by the Clearinghouse, which would lower your GPA in your core courses.

Here's how it works. Your high school is required to send a list of its courses to the Clearinghouse for approval. The Clearinghouse then sends back the list with each course approved or not approved. Your courses must be among those that are approved. This means that if your thirteen core courses average the minimum requirement, but one of them is not approved by the Clearinghouse, you are out of luck. You will not be awarded a scholarship, and you will not be eligible to play. This is not as difficult to achieve as it sounds. If you count up your core curriculum courses, and you have been taking college prep courses all through high school, you should already have the requirements by the end of your junior year. If you are short one or two of these courses for some reason, you have your senior year to include them.

Most students who have maintained a C average in college prep courses are going to have no difficulty being approved by the Clearinghouse. My advice is to go to your guidance counselor and make sure that you have the necessary required courses and the minimum required grade point average in those courses. If you are a junior, you will have a chance to correct any problems you might have. Do this immediately. Don't wait until halfway through your senior year. Remember that your guidance counselor has no way of knowing that you are a potential student athlete or a candidate for a NCAA scholarship to college. It is your responsibility to make him or her aware of this extra requirement for you.

Applications for NCAA Clearinghouse approval should be available through your high school guidance office or through the athletic director. You can also obtain one by calling the NCAA hotline at 1-

800-638-3731. You may apply as early as the spring of your junior year. The latest you should apply is the fall of your senior year. It may take months for your application to be processed through the Clearinghouse.

Your application must be made through the guidance department, just as your college application. You fill out the form and include the required fee and return it to your guidance counselor who will add a copy of your transcript and mail it out for you. Once you have received preliminary approval, your high school will be instructed to send a final transcript upon graduation so that the Clearinghouse has proof of your graduation. You will not be eligible to play without this final approval.

This should give you a pretty fair idea of where you should be playing, you are all registered with the Clearinghouse, and you have sent material out to colleges that interest you. What's next?

First of all, you need to know that there are rules about college coaches contacting players. At any given time it may be prohibited for a college coach to contact you personally. Younger players may only receive general college information in the mail instead of a letter specifically from the coach. You need to be patient. If you are good enough to play for a school's program, the letters and phone calls should follow. In the meantime, you need to send a letter including your statistics and evaluations to the head of each program you are interested in.

Most good coaches prefer to follow up on players they have an interest in by keeping track of their performances in the upcoming season. They also tend to have A-lists and B-lists. Many different colleges are usually recruiting A-list players. Once the early signing period is over (fall of senior year), and after players on the A-list have signed with other schools, the coaches go back to their B-lists and begin to recruit those players. It helps a coach know which players actually have an interest in his or her school.

Although colleges prefer you to apply in the fall, coaches can facilitate your application later in the year if the school still has openings. Final housing deposits usually don't have to be made until May, and we have seen many players make a college decision in the summer after their senior year after being recruited by a coach. You should, however, have SATs sent to any schools you think you might consider. This is necessary to get the ball rolling at any school. Also, if you are not already in the process of applying to schools and have not been contacted by any, please submit some preliminary applications so not to miss out on the opportunity to attend college in the fall.

Once you are contacted by a coach and have established a dialogue, you may find the following list of questions helpful in your discussions and in making a decision. These are the types of questions I would be asking if I were thinking about attending a specific school.

Questions To Ask Coaches

How many players do you currently have at my position?
How many players are you bringing in at my position?
Realistically what are my chances of starting? 50-50? 60-40?
What do you see as my role on the team this year?
What changes do you feel you must make in my hitting or pitching mechanics? Why?
Do you have a pitching coach? What is his philosophy? What does he think of my mechanics?
Do you have a hitting coach? What is his philosophy? What does he think of my style/swing?
As a coach, what things do you feel I must change or improve upon to be successful in your program?
What kind of weight room is available to players?
Are workouts mandatory?
Is there a strength and conditioning coach or trainer available?

Other Questions To Ask That Revolve Around Academics

How difficult will it be to play ball and succeed academically in my desired major?

How much time will I need to spend on baseball in the fall-winter-spring?
How much time does the average player spend on homework each night?
What kind of academic help is available to players?
What happens when the team is away?
Do you have any required team study halls? Are they supervised?
What can be done if a player is really struggling academically?
What GPA will I need to maintain my scholarship?

You'll also need to have answers to all the questions you'll be asked by the specific school. As a rule you'll be asked the same information over and over: social security number, class rank, intended major, SAT or ACT scores, recent statistics, recommendations from coaches and scouts who have seen you play, coach's names and phone numbers and e-mail addresses.

Remember that whenever a coach sends you a letter with a form, it is important to return it promptly, even if the school isn't one of your top choices. It is important to never burn any bridges. Things sometimes don't work out the way you would like them to, and you may have set your sights on a particular program and then things fall through at the last minute. You want to be able to go back to the other coaches who contacted you and try again. Yes it is a lot of trouble, but it is worth the trouble to end up with one college coach who really wants you. If you put all your information in one spot, you may even be able to get a parent or sibling to help you fill out all those forms. When you fill out the forms, write legibly and neatly. Don't return forms that are dirty or smudged. Make a copy of the form if you have to, and send it in.

If a college coach sends you a letter and a form to fill out as well as an application to his school, that is really a good sign. Fill out the application and send it in. Drop a note to the coach who mailed it to you. If he writes on it *fee waiver*, it means he is allowing you to apply to the college without paying an application fee. If he doesn't, and you can't afford all those different school fees, fill out the application anyway, and send it to the coach with a note that you are very interested but can't afford the fee right now, and see what happens.

If you get a phone call from a college coach or scout, don't be scared. Just talk to him and hear what he has to say. Answer his questions as well as you can. If he asks you if you're interested in his school, say yes unless you have definite scholastic goals (pre-med.) and you know his school doesn't offer the course of study you need. Also don't worry about the conversation. Coaches are used to speaking with high school players who don't talk much.

Once you've made your final decision, it is important to drop a note to the other coaches and admission officers you've been in contact with. Just drop them a short note or e-mail thanking them for their help and interest, but tell them you've decided on college X. It is important not to burn your bridges, because it may not work out at college X, and you may have an interest in transferring down the road. (The NCAA also has a complete guidebook on transfers.) If you never sent back their forms, or were not courteous enough to answer them in any way, they will probably tell you to take a hike. However, if you made a good impression on them and they were impressed by your follow up, they might just be willing to help you out.

Keep in mind these are only suggestions and observations we have made over the years of negotiations between our own players and college coaches. The most important thing is to use common sense. You are trying to accomplish something very important: to get all, or part of your college education paid through baseball. This could be worth literally tens of thousands of dollars over four years. This may not mean much to you right now, but it certainly is very important to your parents. And one more thing, if you are fortunate enough to achieve a baseball scholarship, do yourself a favor and study. Stay in school. Keep your eligibility. It will take a great deal of work on your part if you are trying to play ball at the same time, but what a waste to give it up! You worked hard to get where you are and you owe it yourself to give it your best. Good luck.

2001 All-American Baseball Talent Showcases -- Player Ratings + Baseball Tools Measurements

National Director: Joe Barth, Jr., 6 Bicentennial Court, Erial, NJ 08081 Showcases: 855-424-5875 Hit Doctor Baseball Academy: 855-424-8065 Home Office: 855-627-5283

Recently, by recommendation, this player was invited to participate in one of our All-American Baseball Talent Showcases. We have measured and rated his baseball tools numerically, based on his performance at the Showcase.

GENERAL NATIONAL PLAYER RATING SCALE
Pitchers or Arm Comments Key: LC=Little Carry, C=Carry (C-,C-,C++)
A= Consistent Accuracy (Catchers)

1 – 3	Below average.
4	Average high school player.
5 – 6	Above Average to Well Above Average high school player.
7 – 8	Well Above Ave high school plyr to high school Superstar.
9 –10	Pro prospect.

BASIS FOR PITCHERS (MPH +/- Ball Movement)		BASIS FOR CATCHERS ARM (Pop To Pop +/- Accuracy)		BASIS FOR IF/OF ARM (MPH +/- Carry, Accuracy, Rhythm)		BASIS FOR 60's TIMES	
64 or < =1	79-80 = 6	2.70-2.78 = 1	2.20-2.29 = 6	<64 = 3	78-81 = 7	7.71> = 1	7.11-7.30 = 6
65-69 = 2	81-83 = 7	2.60-2.69 = 2	2.11-2.19 = 7	64-69 = 4	82-83 = 8	7.61-7.70 = 2	6.91-7.10 = 7
70-72 = 3	84-85 = 8	2.50-2.59 = 3	2.01-2.10 = 8	70-74 = 5	84-85 = 9	7.51-7.60 = 3	6.71-6.90 = 8
73-74 = 4	86-87 = 9	2.40-2.49 = 4	1.91-2.00 = 9	75-77 = 6	86-87+=10	7.41-7.50 = 4	6.61-6.70 = 9
75-77 = 5	88-90+=10	2.30-2.39 = 5	1.90 or < = 10			7.31-7.40 = 5	6.60 < = 10

PLAYER EVALUATION   2001 SITE # _____ at _____

Site	Pit#	FIRST NAME	LAST NAME	Pos 1	Pos 2	Age	DOB	Grad Yr	HT	WT	Bats	Throws

Street Address	City	ST	Zip Code	Home Phone #	High School	HS Phone #	GPA	PSAT	SAT	ACT

FB MPH	FB Rate	FB Comment	CB MPH	CB Rate	CB Comment	OS MPH	OS Rate	OS Comment

HIT	POWER	ARM	Average Pop to Pop	MPH	FIELD or Catcher RCV	Run 60

OVERALL RATING

Present Pos 1	Projected Pos 1
Present Pos 2	**Projected Pos 2**

General Comments

Joe Barth, Jr.

The Hit Doctor®
Cherry Hill, New Jersey

Considered one of the finest coaches and instructors in America today, Joe Barth, Jr., is a former catcher for College Baseball Hall of Fame Coach, Tom Petroff's Rider University Broncos. Joe has been coaching baseball since 1972, and has coached at every level. In 1978-79, he coached St. Joe's High School baseball team in Camden, New Jersey, reviving their dying program in a single season. When St. Joe's closed its doors the following year, Joe joined legendary Gloucester Catholic High School Rams coach, Al Radano as assistant coach. Several players from St. Joe's followed him there (Bob Sebra - Philadelphia Phillies, Steve Cordner - Cubs, Keith Kowalski - SS/UVA) to round out what many observers feel was the greatest high school team in New Jersey's history: the 1980 Team of the Decade – 25-0, ranked Number One in New Jersey, and Number Two in the Nation.

As great as that was, Joe's passion was the powerhouse Brooklawn Post 72 American Legion – a team with a proud fifty-year tradition. His devotion to Brooklawn began when Joe was four years old in 1951, (the year his father, Joe Sr., *Pop*, founded the team). Brooklawn was a way of life for the entire Barth family and Joe, the oldest of four sons, was the batboy in 1964 when Brooklawn made its very first trip to the American League World Series. For three years Joe assisted his father, working with the pitchers and catchers in the bullpen and in 1981, he began coaching Brooklawn's third base full-time. Brooklawn Legion is recognized nationwide as one of the finest baseball programs in the country. During Joe's twenty years with Brooklawn, the team posted sixteen of their twenty-two New Jersey State Championships (five-times Runner-up), and seven of their nine Regional Championships.

Joe began running camps for players in 1984, and established the Hit Doctor® camps, in 1989. He opened the first Hit Doctor Academy in Cherry Hill, New Jersey, in 1993 and launched the first

All-American Baseball Talent Showcase that same year. The Hit Doctor® camps have been an overwhelming success from coast to coast. Always dedicated to maintaining the highest quality of instruction, Joe believes in keeping the fun in the game he loves. One of his primary goals in life is to help restore the game of baseball to its former stature as America's greatest pastime. He believes that teaching kids the proper way to play, thereby enabling them to enjoy some measure of success, will naturally instill in their hearts a love for the greatest game ever invented.

The Hit Doctor® camps address every facet of the game of baseball, with instructional techniques and drills unlike anything the average player has ever seen. Joe is probably best known for the comprehensive, individualized training system he has developed for hitters, far beyond anything normally offered in a camp situation. It is designed so that, when a player participates in a Hit Doctor® hitting camp, he emerges with a workable program he can stay with for the rest of his career.

The Hit Doctor® camps are always evolving. In the off-season, Joe and some members of his staff travel all over the United States with the All-American Baseball Talent Showcases (nationwide prospect camps for talented high school players), talking and working with professional and college coaches. They bring home their favorite ideas and drills at each position from the top coaches in the country, so that the Hit Doctor® programs always remain fresh and current - what they consider to be the ultimate training programs for young players.

Joe has published articles in *Collegiate Baseball*, produced a series of instructional video tapes on hitting, developed a personalized video capture swing analysis for hitters, and developed the *Throw-Rite Trainer*, a training device for pitchers and position players, originally developed to teach pitchers how to throw breaking pitches. This has evolved into a unique training device used to teach the correct way to throw and increase velocity for all position players.

A popular speaker, Joe is often invited by youth baseball associations to speak at mini-camps and clinics for players and coaches. He has most recently been a guest speaker at the 2001 Minnesota High School Coaches Convention and the 2001 ABCA National

Coaches Convention in Orlando, FL.

You can find out more about Hit Doctor® programs, including the All-American Showcases, at <u>http://www.thehitdoctor.com</u> or call toll-free at 1-800-HIT DOCTor (800-448-3628) for a brochure.

CHAPTER 3

What Professional Scouts Look For

Jay Weitzel
Scout, Minnesota Twins

Picking ballplayers that will be successful at the major league level is not an exact science. In fact, if we are right on one out of ten, we are probably pretty successful. Professional baseball is a very tough sport. Injuries knock out 40% of the prospects, and low pay and time away from family and friends probably takes another 30%. Picking a player who will survive is a difficult chore to say the least; however, we all give it our best shot.

Last year I wrote reports on 40 players. This was my draft list. These were players that I thought could handle the rigors of professional baseball. These were the players I thought had the work ethic to make it in the big leagues. These players came from high school and college.

Every scout has his own grading system, but we all rate physical abilities on pretty much the same scale. One scout might have a 2 to 8 scale and another a 20 to 80 scale, but they all boil down to pretty much the same thing. On the following page is a copy of our *free agent report card,* and I'll break it down column by column. This will give you a good idea of how the average scout rates players as professional prospects.

Positional Players

Hitting Ability

The first area of grading for positional players is hitting ability. We rate with a present and future grade. For most high school players, or players under 18 who have never swung a wood bat, we will grade them a 2. In other words, if we send this player to the minors and he has to face major league pitchers, he will probably hit .200 or under. Now if someone is hitting .400 in the Cape Cod Wood Bat League, we will probably move him up to a 3. Most high school players, however, are a 2, and many college players are a 3 to 4 at present.

We also look at several other aspects when it comes to hitting. We like to see a hitter make the bat whistle through the zone. Guys who do not have good bat speed will not make it to the pros. Bat speed is very important, and if a player has that, we can try to teach him a lot of the rest.

We also look at his swing plane, in and out of the zone. How long is his swing? Does he get the good part of the barrel on the ball, and does he have strike zone awareness? The sweet spot on an aluminum bat is much larger than on a wood bat. (Basically, the aluminum *is* a handle with a sweet spot, whereas wood is a handle with a 3-inch sweet spot.) If the player can't get the sweet spot on the ball with metal, he's going to have a much more difficult time getting it on the sweet spot with wood.

We also look at the mechanics of the swing. Mechanical things we can often fix, but we still pay a lot of attention to them. Running falls under hitting as well. Is he really slow, or can he fly? If he can fly, we might put a 3 on him. Can the player bunt? Does he have enough speed to beat out an infield hit? Good speed will certainly help a player's case.

Free Agent Report Card

(CIRCLE ONE)	AREA	FREE AGENT REPORT		OFP #	ROUND
Draft Follow					

First Report ☐	
Supplemental ☐	Last Name First Name Middle Name

UNIF #_____   AGE _____

Position _____ Bats _____ Throws _____ Hgt _____ Wt. _____ DOB _____

Team Name _____ City _____ State _____

Total Game Seem This Year [   ]   Total Innings Pitched [   ]   Date Last Game Seen [   ]

POSITIONAL PLAYERS	PRES.	FUT.	PITCHERS	PRES.	FUT.
Hitting Ability *			Fast Ball Vel * [ ]		
Raw Power			Fast Ball Mvmt.		
Game Power *			Curve Ball *		
Running Speed * [ ]			Slider * [ ]		
Base Running			Change Up		
Arm Strength *			Other *		
Arm Accuracy			Command		
Fielding *			Control		
Hands			Aggressiveness		
Range			Poise		
Aggressiveness			Instinct		
Instincts			Make Up		
Make Up					

TYPE OF HITTER	DELIVERY
Power Line Drive Slap	OH H3/4 L3/4 SA UH

YR. ELIGIBLE	GRAD DATE

_____ Drive
_____ Set Confidence
_____ Tougness
_____ Pressure Player
_____ Courage
_____ Deduction
_____ Coachability
_____ Work Habits
_____ Off Field Habits

PHYSICAL DESCRIPTION/INJURIES   Glasses _____   Contacts _____   Married   Y   N

_____

_____

_____

STRENGTHS _____

_____

_____

_____

WEAKNESSES _____

_____

_____

_____

OVERALL SUMMATION _____

_____

_____

_____

SIGNABILITY _____

We look closely at the player's strike zone management. Guys that progress don't swing at a curve ball or slider in the dirt. They don't hit from behind in the count, and they try to stay ahead. They don't swing at bad pitches; they make the pitcher pitch to them.

So we start the guy out as a 2 in the present, then we try to project how he'll do in the future. If he has good bat speed, we will move him to a 4. If he has good mechanics, we will move him to a 5. If he can really run, we will go to a 7. Usually we can watch a player take two swings and tell if he can play or not. We know what it is like to face a ball with movement and how you have to run in a game, and because of this, we can evaluate a player very quickly. Being able to assess a player immediately makes a good scout. We have to see so many players that we need to be able to assess their physical attributes very quickly. This is really the easiest part of scouting. Where a good scout really excels is talking to kids and finding out about their inner make-up. Does a ballplayer have what it takes inside to make it to the pros?

Raw Power

Basically, raw power is how far can a player hit a baseball. If a guy can hit a ball out of the park to the opposite field using a wood bat, he has average raw power of about a 5. Very few high school players can consistently do this with a wood bat, so their raw power number will be much lower. Most high school players would get a 2 here.

When we watch high school and college players take batting practice, we have to account for smaller parks, so we try to evaluate body type and bat speed. Raw power is a real important grade, and it will get you noticed.

Game Power

Game power is different than raw power. We are trying to make an educated guess as to how many home runs that we think this player could hit in the major leagues. 30+ home runs is an 8 in the big leagues. Major league levels are as follows: A 2 is 0-3 home runs a season. A 3 is 4-6 home runs. A 4 is 7-9 home runs. A 5 is 10-15 home runs. A 6 is 16-22 home runs, and a 7 is 23-29 home runs. If we think you could eventually hit 10-15 home runs in the majors, we would give you a future 5 grade. This is at best an educated guess.

Running Speed

In my opinion, 60-yard dash times aren't that important in baseball, but almost everyone goes by them to a certain extent. Most good scouts can watch the way a kid walks and tell if he can run or not. Some kids run a great 60 but it doesn't play into the game because they don't have that quick first step. When you analyze it, the most a player will usually have to run in a straight line is about 40 yards if he is a center fielder. We often look at his time from home to first, which is very important. From the right side a 4.2 runner would be a 6. We also look at instincts. You need them to steal bases. Running time is usually pretty hard to get to go down, but easy to go up. Ballplayers get heavier and more muscular, and then they begin to slow down causing speed times to level off or go higher.

Running is a money tool and every team can use it because you never have slumps in speed. To us a 6.6 sixty is an 8, a 6.7 is a 7. Home to first from the right side: a 4.0 or lower is an 8, a 4.1 is a 7. From the left side: A 3.9 is an 8, a 4.0 is a 7.

Base Running

This refers basically to stolen bases. An 8 grade in the majors is 35+ steals. 25-34 is a 7, 16-24 is a 6, 12-15 is a 5, 6-11 is a 4, and 2-6 is a 3. This is something that can improve. Once a player learns the pitchers and learns how to burst in his running to steal bases, he will get better at this. What we look at now is: Does the player study pitchers? Does he do the little things that will allow him to get better, or is he a dumb runner? A good base runner is a very valuable commodity for a team.

Arm Strength

What we look for in arm strength is very little gravity on the ball. Does a third baseman's throw stay up all the way across the diamond? For an outfielder, we like to see a straight throw directly to the base in the air or on one hop. We don't want to see a dead hop either. We want to see an accelerated hop to give a guy a 5 or 6 grade.

We can put a 5 on most good arms, but we have to say *wow* to give a guy a 6. Usually a guy who has a 5 arm can throw 85 or 86 off the mound. A 6 would mean 88 or so, and a 92 would grade out at an 8. In order to check a catcher's arm strength, we would have him throw stationery, straddling home plate to second from a set position. The average catcher's pop-time in the majors is 1.85. Most high school catchers are around 2.00.

Arm Accuracy

Arm accuracy isn't that important because it is something that can be improved and worked on. If they have arm strength, we can work with them to improve their throwing accuracy.

Fielding

Does a player have good range and soft hands? Can he go get the ball? Is his technique clean? Does he know what he is doing? How is his exchange from glove to throwing position? You don't have to have great running speed, but your first step must be clean and quick. When he takes his first step, he should land on the ball of his foot, not his heel. A fielder's first step is very important, whether he is playing second base or center field.

Aggressiveness

Good ballplayers can't sit back and succeed. They need to be aggressive throughout the entire game. We look and see if a kid is backing off the plate on a guy with a good fastball, or does he hang in there by challenging the pitcher to put one by him? Will the guy hang in there at second base with a 230-pounder breathing down his neck? Is the base runner taking an aggressive lead, or is he being too conservative? These are the things we look for.

Instincts

Instincts revolve around a player's feel for the game. Is he always in position? Does he know where to go? Does he know how to take the extra base? Is he always backing up the play? Can he read the batter's swing so he gets a better jump on the ball?

Make-Up

This is one of the most important lines on the whole report. We need to know a player's drive. Does he have self-confidence? Is he a pressure player? Does he have courage? Is he dedicated? Is he coachable or is he a real know-it-all? What are his work ethics and off-field habits?

You find out quickly just how tough you are when you get smacked with the ball and you taste your own blood. Pressure players can hit the home run when the score is 2-1 and bases are loaded. They don't strike out. Players who get RBIs are pressure guys.

Does he really love baseball? Does he show up on time and dress properly? Is he always a problem? Does he always forget his shirt if his mother doesn't put it in his bag? Can he listen? You have two ears and one mouth. A player learns more by listening. What are his work habits? Does he take the minimum number of ground balls, or does he ask you for more? Does he go to the weight room every day or just scheduled days? Does he take the minimum number of swings, or does he try and take more? Does he get adequate sleep, or is he up late every night? What are his eating habits? Is his nutrition good?

Every day a player has to keep improving himself. He has to get bigger and stronger and better. A player needs a special make-up to be able to do this.

Pitchers

Fast Ball Velocity

For pitchers, first and foremost, we look at velocity. At what speed does he consistently throw his fastball? We will then look at his physical make-up and see if he still has room for growth. If he has a projectable body and is throwing 88 MPH, we will look at him. Especially if he works his butt off and listens to instruction. Grading here is usually pretty close to present score. If he is throwing 88, he's a present 4. If he has room to grow, I might put a future 5 on him, which would be 89-91. If he is 96+, he is an 8, 94-95 a 7, 92-93 a 6, 89-91 a 5, 87-88 a 4, 85-86 a 3, and 84 or under a 2.

If a player hasn't had much coaching from a pitching perspective and perhaps never had a real long-toss program, but has a body that can add weight and strength and throws 84-85, we will follow him. He has some potential to get better.

Fast Ball Movement

As for the fastball itself, we look to see how many bats the pitcher is missing. Are other players getting good swings at his fastball? Hitters will tell you if the pitcher has any movement or *stuff* on the ball. Radar guns tell you how fast he is throwing. But hitters tell you how much movement the pitcher has by the number of pitches they are missing. A guy throwing 85-86 with good movement on his fastball may be a better prospect than the guy throwing 89-90 with zero movement.

Curveball

When we look at a player's curveball, we see how it spins. Does the ball tumble? Does it snap down? Does it work easy? We don't like the ones that stay on the same plane. Is it difficult to hit? Does it break late and tight, or is it a floater that everyone can see? What velocity does he throw it at? We usually like to see a curve about 10 MPH slower than the pitcher's fast ball.

Slider

Not many high school or college pitchers have a good slider. If a kid throws a good slider around 80 MPH, he is a prospect. Most pitchers throw this off a low elbow. We like to see the elbow up and going through two planes.

Change-Up

Late movement and no discernable difference in arm speed is the key here. It has to look like a fastball. To be a starter he will need a solid change-up to disrupt the hitter's timing.

Other

Does he throw a split finger? A knuckleball? A cutter? A slurve? When he throws it, is it effective?

Command

This refers to being able to put a ball where you want it. Can the pitcher put the curveball where he wants it? It is not that easy to put pitches where you want them to go. Most everyone has a 2 to start. Greg Maddux is an 8. He could knock a fly off a dog's butt at 60 feet 6 inches. It is very important in pitching to put the ball where you want. Pitchers with poor command make too many mistakes and give up too many home runs.

Control

Control is based on an average nine-inning game, and based on future projections. Big league control is walking less than 3 hitters every nine innings. This would be a 5. An 8 is 1 ½ per nine innings, and a 2 is 5 per nine innings.

A pitcher needs to remember that the higher you go in baseball, that more things favor the hitters. The strike zones are a lot smaller (about the size of a postage-stamp.) The lights are better. The umpires are better. If you can't put the ball where you want to now, you are going to have a very difficult time later.

Aggressiveness

Does he go after hitters? Does he pitch inside?

Poise

Does he have a lot of balks? Does he throw his glove? A pitcher needs to be able to handle adverse situations. Can he gather himself up and start over with the next batter? Does he have damage control?

Physical Description

In summary we give a physical description of the player. We start from the ankles and work our way up from there. Does he have a good frame? Is he overweight or underweight? Are his arms strong? Does he have large hands or feet? Does he have a short torso? Will his body hold up through a rigorous professional season?

Strengths/Weaknesses

When we get to strengths and weaknesses, we list and profile five basic tools. The tools are fielding, throwing, hitting, power and running.

For each position there is a different order of priorities.

A Catcher:	Field, Throw, Hit, Power and Run.
A Left Fielder:	Hit, Power, Run, Field and Throw
A Center Fielder:	Run, Field, Throw, Hit and Power

First and third, and left and right are hitting positions. In center field, hitting isn't such a big issue, but you need to be able to run, field and throw well.

Overall Summary

When we get to overall summation, this is where I project a player to be in the big leagues. If I am going to write him up as a money player with all the tools, he is going to be an 8 overall. A 7 will probably be a quality, important player with some all-star years in there. A 6 is a solid starter that maybe lacks one particular tool. A 5 is an average player offensively and defensively, but a regular. A 4 is a platoon player or maybe a pinch hitter who can hit or play a little. Maybe we like his bat or his glove. A low 4 or 4-minus may be a defensive player or a back-up player. A 3 is a fringe player who may be a back-up only. He may do one or two things well, but not others. This player might make it, but only as a backup. A 2 is someone we don't think can play in the majors.

It is almost impossible to turn in an 8. We would really be putting our necks out there. If we turn in a 7, other scouts in the organization will probably check him out as well.

Overall it is tremendously satisfying to be able to locate and sign a player who eventually will make it to the majors. It is important to realize that less than one-half percent of all high school players will get drafted. That is one out of every two hundred. The odds are slim, but if you work hard and have some natural ability, you could end up being that 1 in 200 player who gets drafted.

Jay Weitzel

Professional Baseball Scout
Minnesota Twins

Jay Weitzel has been an Area Scout for the Minnesota Twins since 1998. His love for sports, as well as his ability to communicate effectively with the athletes, has been the key to his success.

Born and raised in Salamanca, New York, Jay played baseball and football in high school and college. He received his degree from Canisius College in New York, and later joined a fast pitch softball league, where he played in the Fast Pitch World Series four times in Florida and Virginia and twice in Ohio. For the next eleven years he scouted for football, and conducted baseball camps for players.

In 1997, Jay joined the Pittsburg Pirates as an Associate Scout in the Jacksonville, Florida, area. Just a year later in 1998, he went to New York to work for the Minnesota Twins as an Area Scout for the East Coast. The Twins wanted a scout who could assess a player accurately and efficiently, and Jay was able to do this for them. His position requires him to travel from high schools, to colleges, to instructional leagues and to minor league baseball games. Anywhere there is a possible recruit, Jay is there to assess the potential player.

Jay attributes much of his success to individuals he calls *Role Molders*, such as George Whitcher and Tom Hershey (his football coaches), Dusty Rhodes of the University of North Florida, and his parents, Bill and Judy.

Jay lives in Pennsylvania with his wife, Robin and two sons, Adam and Jerico, as well as Kaiser, his German Shepherd.

You can reach Jay at the Minnesota Twins, 1431 Treasure Lake, Dubois, PA 15801 or E-mail him at jayweitzel@twinsbaseball.com.

CHAPTER 4

College Or Pro?

Tom Rizzi
College Select Baseball, LLC

You are now a high school senior and are hoping to make your baseball dream come true: to take your game to the next level, college or pro.

Will you be one of the few lucky ones who go on and play college ball?

Will you be one of the even fewer lucky ones who will get drafted right out of high school and go pro?

The odds of both are slim, but pro ball odds are the slimmer of the two. Keeping this in mind we will look at how you should approach your high school baseball career to make it work for you (as a *plus tool*) to get you to the next step.

I am an education advocate and firmly believe that even if you want to play pro baseball, the education element is critical. Baseball players do not play forever, and one pitch or one play can end a career even before it begins. Even for those who make it to the *big leagues,* the life span of a major league player is not that long. I personally would prefer it if major league baseball not draft kids out of high school. I do not believe many of those drafted at the ages of seventeen or eighteen are ready to deal with the physical and psychological pressures of professional baseball. In my opinion players have a better chance to succeed if drafted after two years of junior college or after their junior year of a four-year school. However, your goal as a player is to get to the next level, whether that may be college or pro.

As a high school baseball player your first priority should be getting good grades because baseball money at colleges (despite all the stories you may have heard), is minimal. Good academics can help you get into a financial situation that your family can handle. I call it easing the burden. As you go into your senior year of high school make sure that you get the NCAA Clearinghouse Forms necessary to play college ball. You should be able to obtain these from your guidance counselor. *If you do not get approved by the Clearinghouse, you cannot play Division I or Division II College Baseball.*

In an effort to assist the players in this process, at College Select Baseball we purchase NCAA Clearinghouse booklets and give them to the players at our showcases as part of the showcase package. The NCAA Clearinghouse is a key element for getting scholarships for baseball in college. At the latest the registration form should be sent to the NCAA Clearinghouse the first week you get back to school in your senior year. Final approval by the NCAA Clearinghouse does not come until after your final high school transcript is accepted. Prior to this you will receive partial or temporary approval, which lets college coaches know that you are a viable prospect. This also applies to the pro baseball aspect because if you are a top prospect and are not cleared, or are questionable with regard to the NCAA Clearinghouse, it will change how a pro team looks at you for the draft. Thus, you can see that your academic standing not only affects your choices for college but also how the pro teams look at you. It is your responsibility to obtain the academic requirements necessary to open the doors to college or pro baseball. If you are not a sure-fire pro prospect, then you want to be certain that you have the alternative of playing college ball. The better the academics, the more alternatives you will have.

Another item of importance regarding the NCAA Clearinghouse is the Core Curriculum required. It differs a bit from what most colleges/universities ask for. For example, the Clearinghouse requires one year of a language while most colleges/universities require two. Rather than go into a long and tedious discourse on the requirements let me direct you to the NCAA web site, *www.ncaa.org* where you can read it all for yourself.

We all know how hard it is to make it as a pro player. Now with the possibility of lowering the number of draft rounds, it may become even more difficult. Each team has its own thoughts and practices on who and how to draft. Some like to take college players because they feel they are more physically and psychologically mature. Others like to draft high school players because they feel they can influence them more and turn them into the player they want. There is no easy formula for these Major League teams just as there is no easy formula for players as to the decision whether to go pro or to college. It is a difficult question, and the answer will not be the same for each player. Each player's situation stands on its own merit. Hopefully when you complete this chapter you will have a better understanding of what it entails and this, in turn, may help you make a good decision.

Let's start with something that might put the entire picture into perspective – a pitcher who throws 90 MPH plus. Research any of the Internet baseball sites and you will see stories of pitchers who throw 90 MPH. However in reality, pro scouts state that there are only approximately 60 such arms in college and maybe only 40 such arms in high school. Thus at the maximum there are approximately 100 pitchers in the entire country who throw 90 MPH or better on a regular basis. And yes, pro scouts are eyeballing these few players. College coaches try to sign pitchers of this magnitude, but they know the odds are against them with pro scouts also making offers. Don't get me wrong, some of these kids will attend college because that is what is important to them, but the majority will be drafted and sign a pro contract.

Following are a few options besides academics that you may want to participate in during high school to get maximum exposure from both pro scouts and college coaches alike.

Travel Teams: This is one way of getting seen. It can be an expensive route, but in the end I think you will find it to be well worth the investment. Playing on a team such as this enables you to play with, and against, top caliber players. It will help you to improve your game as well as give you an idea as to where your talent stands in comparison to that of others. It will also get you seen by scouts and coaches, as they will attend these games more than any other types of games. Most travel teams spend the majority of their time playing in tournaments or showcases so coaches and scouts can attend and see numerous players of equal talent all at the same time.

Showcases: At showcases you get exposure as an individual, not as a team member. At a showcase you will get the opportunity to demonstrate your skills to the array of coaches and pro scouts in attendance. You will run the 60-yard dash; you will get to show your arm strength. As a catcher they will time your throws to second (pop times), and pitchers will be timed by radar guns from the pitcher's mound. In many instances you will also take batting practice.

You can also include pro team tryout camps in this section. Regional pro scouts or the Major League Scouting Bureau run these events. They are open to players usually between the ages of 16 and 26. College coaches, as well as pro scouts usually attend them, so it becomes a good means of exposure. It will also open a player's eyes to see how many players have the same dream as they do. You will see men 24, 25 and 26 years old still holding on to the dream of playing pro baseball.

You can find schedules for tryouts on the respective web sites of all the Major League teams. It is also possible that you will get a personal invitation to attend. Take your wood bat with you when you go; they don't want to see you hit with aluminum.

Fall Leagues: Since college coaches are busy with their own seasons in the spring, fall has become a key time for high school players to be seen by college coaches. In the fall coaches and pro scouts can concentrate on seeing high school players in action. Fall leagues have now become almost as popular as *select* teams in the summer. There are even travel teams in the fall that take part in weekend tournaments as well as team showcase events. I have found that these events give a player great exposure. We have a College Select Team made up of players from our showcase events and we enter as many of these fall events as possible. We do not have many weekends off from September to the beginning of November.

Wood Bat Leagues: If you have pro baseball dreams, then you want to play in a wood bat league and be seen by pro scouts. Since high school and college baseball are played with aluminum bats and pro ball uses wood, this is where the pro scouts can get an idea how you hit with wood in hand. We at College Select have gone to wood bat batting practice sessions at our showcases so that the coaches and scouts can assess how you hit with wood versus how you hit with aluminum.

All four of the above mentioned venues will get you great exposure whether or not you are thinking pro or college for your next level of baseball. Keep in mind that high school baseball is nice, but in the spring, college coaches are into their own schedules so they do not have the time to see you play. Thus it is critical to play outside of the high school season to be seen and gain exposure.

The above four means of being seen, in addition to your high school games, serve both the college coaches and the pro scouts. There is nothing you do to be seen by one group that does not get you seen by the other. College coaches attend even pro tryout camps, so you again have one venue for both, college and pro.

Let us now get into some particular questions that may help you make that all-important decision – how do I choose between college and pro ball.

How Do Scouts And College Coaches Get To Know Me?

With Internet exposure and all the showcase and recruiting programs for players, it is not too hard to get known – for either good or bad reviews. Most programs have Internet web sites that list players, and some even go so far as to *rate and rank* players.

What Do Statistics Do For Me?

At the end of the day statistics mean nothing. Until such time as all players face the same level of competition, high school statistics really are non-consequential in a coach or scout's eyes. Even the honors, All League, All Section, All County, and All State can be incidental because they can at times be politically skewed.

Am I Eligible For The Draft?

As I am writing this, the following are eligible for the draft.
- ◆ Graduating high school seniors.
- ◆ Junior college players.
- ◆ Players who have completed their third year of college.
- ◆ Players age 21 years within 45 days of the draft date.
- ◆ Special circumstance players, *(i.e.* dropped out of school) can be granted eligibility by submitting a request and stating the facts to the Baseball Commissioner's Office by specific dates prior to the draft.

Do Pre-Draft Workouts Mean Anything At All?

If you are a high school player, make sure your State Federation Rules permit you to take part in pro tryout camps.

In my opinion if there are more than a dozen players attending a Pre-Draft workout, it is not a great opportunity for you. It really only means something if there are fewer than a dozen players attending, but even then, it does not mean you will be drafted.

What Increases Your Chances Of Being Drafted?

God-given talent and the drive to succeed and improve increase your chances of being drafted. Many will tell you that playing at a high profile college will increase your chances, but that is not necessarily so. If you are a good player on the college level, scouts will find you. If you are in high school and do the things we spoke of earlier in terms of being seen, they will find you. To me however, the key element that can set you apart from all the others is your drive to succeed and hustle – even when running on and off the field.

When Is The Best Time To Be Drafted?

Again this goes back to individual beliefs. As we said earlier some teams like high school players because they can mold them while others like college players because they are more mature and developed. But what is best for you? Are you ready to take ten-hour bus rides at the rookie level? Are you ready to be one of the few English-speaking kids on a team? It can be quite a culture shock for some young men. Many are not ready for this sort of life at the age of 17 or 18. If you are a very low draft pick, there is not a lot of up-front money to be found, and the $850/900 you get paid as a rookie does not go very far after taxes and rent are taken out. Are you ready for that sort of life?

On the other hand if you are a pro draft prospect, the college programs pursuing you will be top flight, and travel and living in a major college baseball program can help you mature. In addition, once you are in a four-year program, you cannot be drafted until after your junior year or you have turned 21. So you should have three years of college under your belt, making it easier to complete your degree if you get drafted out of college as a junior.

Another factor is family financial needs. The huge signing bonus in some cases can be a needed salvation for the family finances. In this case it really becomes a no-brainer in terms of going pro or not going pro. If the family needs funds, and you can get a six figure signing bonus or larger, then it is very hard to say no. For others money may not be a factor.

It has become standard for college tuition to be tied into signing money, but one must know the stipulations that are involved. There can be a time period and maximum dollars per semester involved. All the small print has to be read and re-read.

I believe that if you are drafted out of high school, the signing bonus should be upwards of $750,000 or you don't sign. If you get drafted after three years of college, the dollar figure can be a lot less. But again this is my personal belief and every family situation stands on its own merit.

Remember also that if drafted out of high school you have until the first day you attend class to sign. It is not something that you have to rush into.

What it truly comes down to is what does the player want? Some players and their parents have had a life long dream: that *Johnny boy* play pro ball. Other families consider a college education a priority, and they will not sign unless the pro signing bonus figures are in the $700,000 range. There are also the players who are not college material academically. This can hurt them in pro negotiations due to the lack of a bargaining chip – the college scholarship.

What About An Agent/Advisor?

If you think that you are going to be a high draft pick and the money will be six figures, then you may want to have someone negotiate the signing bonus with you (such as a counselor, advisor or agent). If you are a very late draftee, then you don't need an agent because the money is not large enough to warrant giving away up to twenty percent of it.

So What Are We Saying Here?

We are saying that you should prepare yourself in high school for a college baseball career. This assures you of being in a position to go on to college if the pro option does not materialize. The more options that you are capable of having, the stronger your bargaining position will be. You do not want to be in a position that eliminates other options if you are not drafted.

It is not the end of the world if you do not get drafted out of high school. You still have your college career to improve your skills and gain maturity. This is why I stress the importance of education, and it all has to begin at the high school level. If it does not begin at the high school level, then it does not happen at the college level.

So are we saying it is better to go pro out of high school than after college? No.

Are we saying that going pro is a sure means to a pot of gold? No.

Are we saying that going the college route is preferable to going pro? No.

What we are saying is that whatever road you choose, it is not easy, and the number of players involved in this choice is small. Thus you should prepare for every possibility. It is truly a one-time shot for either to happen, and you don't want to blow it by not being prepared for it. You do not want to *have* to go pro because your grades are not good enough for college. You do not want to lose your bargaining power by not having college choices. This is especially so in light of recent talk of revising the draft format.

A player wants to have as many *plus factors* on his side as possible. Remember you cannot control when and who drafts you, but you can control other factors such as academics, work ethic and exposure. If you control what you can, the decision to go pro or go to college will be a lot easier for you if you are one of the select few to be drafted. If you are not drafted out of high school, you will be ready for a fine college baseball career. Take my word for it: There is a college out there for every qualified player if he looks hard enough. It might not be his first choice, but there will be a place for him.

Tom Rizzi

College Select Baseball, LLC

Tom Rizzi's passion for baseball started when his grandmother gave him his first bat and glove as soon as he could walk. From that day on he has loved the game. In high school and college he played baseball until an arm injury ended his career. He then turned to coaching.

While coaching he found a number of players in need of additional assistance with the college selection and recruiting process. As a result, in 1993 he founded the *College Select Baseball Program* in an effort to assist and guide high school players and their parents through this recruiting process. To date, Tom and the College Select Program have helped hundreds of players find their way into college, and have helped a few get recruited by the major leagues. Their niche, however, is college recruitment.

The first College Select Showcase was held at Cubeta Stadium in Stamford, Connecticut in 1994. From that one event the College Select Baseball Program has grown into one of the most respected and highly recognized showcase programs in the country.

In the year 2002, College Select grew to five showcases held in Norwich, Connecticut; Brooklyn, New York; Binghamton, New York; Lakewood, New Jersey; and Fresno, California. Other College Select venues include a major tournament showcase in East Hartford, Connecticut, and a Select Travel Team that appears in team showcase events in the fall up and down the East Coast.

Tom lives in Connecticut with his wife, Lynne.

You can reach Tom or the College Select Baseball Program by mail at PO Box 783, Manchester, CT 06040, by visiting their website at www.collegeselect.org; by phone at 800-782-3672 or by e-mail at TRhit@msn.com.

CHAPTER 5

The Magic 5%

Jim Vigue
Peak Power Baseball

In the next three chapters we will discuss how to raise your performance level in the three key skill areas of baseball: running, hitting and throwing. As for speed, however, most ballplayers believe they are either born with it or there is little they can do to improve it.

Genetics play a big part in both your physical size and shape. To a certain extent they also help decide whether you have speed or don't have it. Certainly a 6'2" solidly built 225-lb. catcher in high school who currently runs a 7.6 60-yard dash, isn't going to become a 6.5 sprinter by doing a few exercises. You either have a predisposition to speed, or you don't. However, don't get discouraged, because I believe everyone can show some improvement in their basic skill levels by taking part in a comprehensive, well designed program that maximizes his basic genetic inheritance. I will show you that often a minimum of merely a 5% improvement in basic speed levels could make the difference between whether you get a major college scholarship or are noticed by professional scouts. Almost everyone, with the exception of already highly fine-tuned and well-trained athletes, can achieve this 5% improvement by following the advice contained in the following chapters. Let's take a look and see what a 5% improvement might do to various skill levels.

In chapter 8, Karl Schilling writes about why bat speed is important and how to improve it. In his excellent book, *The Physics of Baseball,* Robert K. Adair-Sterling, Professor of Physics at Yale University does an outstanding job of showing how physics affects baseball. It is a fascinating read, and I think one of his most interesting conclusions was that a ball stays on a bat only about 1/1000th of a second. When a ball only spends that much time on a bat, you can see how important it is to generate as much power when you swing as is possible. To see why this generation of bat speed could be important to you, let's look at the following example:

A hitter is facing a pitcher throwing an 85-MPH fastball and the centerfield fence is 400 feet away. Assume there are no other variables such as extreme temperature or high winds, and the player has bat speed of 70 MPH. The hitter swings and hits the ball to centerfield. With bat speed of 70 MPH and a pitched ball speed of 85 MPH, according to Adair's book, the ball will end up being caught by the centerfielder.

Let's assume the hitter works to increase his bat speed and increases it by only 5% to 73.5 MPH. All things being equal, the next time this hitter meets up with this 85-MPH pitcher and hits it solidly, the ball will most likely go over the fence. The 5% improvement is the difference between a long fly out and a home run.

Often it is just a minor improvement that makes the difference between success and failure. The average high school player should be able to improve his bat speed with a comprehensive program by a minimum of 10%.

In his chapter on *How to Throw Harder,* national javelin champion, Tom Pukstys illustrates how to find more throwing power.

If you are a pretty good high school left-handed pitcher throwing an average of 83-84 MPH, you are probably a pretty good pitcher and can probably play at college somewhere. Would a major Division I college or a professional scout be interested in you? Probably not unless they saw a very high ceiling or could fix a couple of obvious mechanical flaws in your delivery. If you go on a concentrated program to increase velocity and you gain roughly 5% in velocity, what does this do for you?

If you are throwing consistently at 83-84 MPH and you increase this by 5%, your velocity then becomes 87-88 MPH. Suddenly you've taken yourself from a small college prospect to a Division I prospect. There are a few top-30 college lefties that are successfully pitching in Division I at 83 or 84 MPH; however, you probably wouldn't get much of a look. But a 5% improvement would make a difference. While a 5% improvement in throwing velocity is harder to achieve than a 5% improvement in bat speed, it is achievable by most athletes who spend the necessary time on it.

My son, Kris, was a perfect example. At a showcase at the end of his sophomore year he threw 83 MPH. Not bad, but not hard enough to get much attention. At the beginning of his senior year at another showcase, with a little over a year of training, he threw and hit 88 MPH. At 88 MPH college scouts started giving him a second look.

Ed Ruisz has written an excellent chapter on how to increase running speed. Speed is very important to most top college programs and of utmost importance to major league programs. Major league teams realize that sometimes a little extra speed makes the difference between catching a long fly ball or not, or beating out an infield grounder or not. The average major league runner does the 60-yard dash in around 6.9 or 7 seconds. That's the average major leaguer. As we saw in Jay Weitzel's chapter, *What Professional Scouts Look For,* if you run a 6.6 sixty, you are going to receive their highest rating.

Perhaps you are running a 6.9 sixty and playing centerfield. This isn't bad. You are running at the major league average, but it isn't at a speed that is really going to get you noticed. You begin a comprehensive running program that is designed to increase your stride length and stride rate. Let's say that working diligently on this program smoothes out your running mechanics and gains you a 5% improvement in your 60-yard dash speed. Suddenly, your okay 6.9 is an attention grabbing 6.55. At 6.5 seconds, colleges and the pros will notice you. Only a 5% improvement, but a major difference.

The same holds true for home-to-first times. A 5% improvement here often means the difference between beating out a ground ball or not. A good 4.2 time from the left side of the plate becomes a below 4 second time.

Perhaps not magic, but I think you get the idea that only a minor improvement could make a tremendous difference in your success as a ballplayer. A slight improvement in foot speed or a slight difference in throwing velocity or bat speed could mean the difference in whether or not you move to the next level of baseball. Little things, little differences, little mental edges, and little improvements in velocity or speed can make all the difference in the world. It will take some effort, but if you achieve that magic 5% improvement, it will be well worth it.

Jim Vigue

Former USA Baseball Amateur
Coach of the Year - Maine
Longwood, Florida

Jim Vigue has been involved in youth sports for over thirty years. In 1997 he was named USA Baseball's and Major League Player's Association Amateur Coach of the Year from Maine.

Jim moved his family to Florida in 2001 so his son, Kris, could play baseball at a top Florida program and test himself against some of the best competition in the State his senior year of high school. The high school he attended (Lake Mary) was ranked as high as number 5 in the country, and his son's legion team, Post 53, won the State Legion Championship. Kris eventually signed a national letter of intent with a Division I program.

An experienced marketer, Jim is also a founding partner of the Executive Sports Club of Orlando, a private club designed to bring business people and former professional athletes together on a monthly basis. Jim also serves as a consultant to parents assisting them in finding the right college program for their sons through his internet company, *www.peakpowerbaseball.com.*

Jim lives in central Florida with his wife, Ivy, and two children, Kris and Kaily, and their dog, Docket.

To contact Jim, e-mail him at jim@peakpowerbaseball.com or call him at 407-321-6137.

CHAPTER 6

How To Throw Harder

Tom Pukstys
Olympian

Is it possible to improve throwing power and velocity? Yes it is. The goal of this chapter is to offer some insight on the training needed to improve throwing power for all players. You will have to grasp the basics of what a throw is, and how physical training or preparation affects you, but once you have a simple understanding of these things, you will then be able to do something about it.

Almost every thrower wants to improve his power and abilities but often doesn't know where to begin. After reading the following pages, you will have an understanding of where to start, and how far to go.

What Is A Throw?

Throwing any object is actually much more than just an arm movement. No matter what kind of object you throw, and no matter which way you throw it, a throw is a chain reaction of the body that starts with the feet. It is similar to cracking a whip.

If you were to look at a pitcher in slow motion, you would see that the legs begin the action of firing the ball. First the pitcher winds up, or coils, and then the leg on the ground begins a pushing motion to get the lead leg out in front and planted, while a turning motion of the back leg gets the waist to start moving from facing sideways to the throw to facing it directly. Then there is a torque feeling across the stomach and chest as the shoulder and arm are positioned behind. Once the chest faces the target, the arm gets pulled like a rubber band as the shoulder, then elbow, then wrist, fire in a sequence with the ball leaving the finger as if it were shot out of a cannon. The whole body gets used to delivering a pitch.

If you want to increase your throwing power, you can't simply work on the arm. You have to work all the muscles in the chain that makes a throw happen. Any weaknesses and the possibility of injury become real. You should have good power in your legs, but have the flexibility in them to use your waist. Your waist, not just the abs, does a ton of work. It is the transmitter of power from the legs to the upper body, and also has to be your center of gravity. I will usually describe the waist as a whole when I explain about that area, instead of the abs alone. Since the throwing motion is a twisting motion, you have to have a strong and fit lower back, great side muscles, (oblique) and also have front abdominal fitness. You must have the whole package.

The chest and shoulders work together, and they must be flexible and powerful, not tight. The final stage in the release of a ball is the arm. Although having big arms with big muscles may look great, you should still be trying to make your arm fast and flexible so it can reach its potential. The bottom line is this: A throw is an unwinding of the whole body. You have to make it a goal to keep the body fit and flexible to be a great powerful pitcher, or any position player who needs to throw like a rocket.

The Throwing Athlete

Now that you have an understanding of what a throw is, you must define the physical characteristics of the throwing athlete. You are fortunate to have great exposure all summer long to the best baseball players in the game through television and also in person. What you will see are fit athletes who rely on quickness and agility to make a play, and have flexibility and power to make a throw. You can use these stars of the game as your model to shoot for. The goal for all players, and especially pitchers, should be great athleticism, by being flexible and strong over a long range of motion. What you see on the field today defines the athletic goal, and this dictates the type of training you should be doing.

Key Areas To Improve Throwing Ability

There are three areas that enhance your ability to throw with power and precision. The ability to hit a target, the psychology of a strong throw, and the ability to use your legs and waist in the throw.

All young players should spend most of their time trying to improve their ability to hit a target. I don't mean the ability to throw a strike, but a general overall ability to throw any object accurately. Whenever you have a chance, make throwing accurately a game. Make it fun. Try throwing rocks at a can, or a tennis ball through a hoola-hoop. Every young player must first learn to throw accurately before taking a step up to more power.

Another critical aspect in improving throwing power is the psychology of a hard throw. The mindset must be to throw to the target you are throwing at, and throw through it. You have to shatter your target with power, and it starts with your thinking. During an interview with relief pitcher Kyle Farnsworth of the Chicago Cubs, a 103-MPH fastball thrower, I asked him to describe his mindset for a 100-MPH pitch. "I just relax more, and throw it through the catchers mitt," he said, "I don't even think of the hitter; it's like I have tunnel vision." Your strongest throws should be accurate. When you use the mindset of throwing *through* the target, your body will naturally follow through harder, and chase after the throw. Most people can throw harder just by thinking about it.

The final aspect to improve is the ability to use your legs and waist. Your arms have limits to how hard they can throw, but the legs and waist increase these limits if you work on them. Your legs and waist have powerful muscles. Knowing that a throw is a chain reaction, you should increase the speed of the beginning of the action, and the end result should be greater. Training the legs and waist to be used in a throw more efficiently and more powerfully will take a lot of repetitious work. It will take the repetitions for your body to accept the action subconsciously and perform it naturally. You must use your legs without directly thinking about it. Like riding a bicycle, you practice as a child and then when it is comfortable, you get on the bike and ride it without much thought.

There are three areas that are key aspects to work on: the ability to hit a target, the psychology of a strong throw, and the ability to use the lower body.

Training and Workout Requirements

Now that we have defined the areas of focus needed to become a powerful baseball thrower, I will offer you the type of training you should get involved with. Training can be divided into three levels: strength, power, and specific power. Strength is like laying a foundation for the other levels. Strength in itself is useless to an athlete unless he or she does some more aggressive training to make power. Power is strength with speed. Power is what is needed in all sporting activity, but specific power gives an athlete the ability to perform his or her event.

Baseball players will need to spend most of their time training for power and specific power. But without some strength their improvement might not be as dramatic. In order to understand why a baseball player needs to work hard on power movements, you have to know a little about how your muscles operate. If you were to test your maximum strength on the bench press, it would take your muscles about half a second to three-quarters of a second to recruit all the muscle fibers needed to make the lift. In baseball, this amount of time is eternity. A 90-MPH fastball reaches the plate from the mound in four-tenths of a second. You get a couple tenths to read the pitch and a couple tenths to swing at it. At this moment your strength alone won't help you. You will have to be quick and powerful to get the bat around. Having a super high maximum in the bench press might sound cool to you and your friends, but you won't use it when hitting, or throwing, unless you have flexibility and speed.

The reason for training for flexibility and speed is to take advantage of your muscles' ability to use the stretch reflex, an elastic component. It is possible for your muscles to react more powerfully with pre-stretching of the muscle. This whole event is known as the stretch-shortening cycle. Think of your muscle as having some of the characteristics of a rubber band. If you stretched out your muscles and tendons, there is the ability for those tissues to store elastic energy. If your muscles begin to contract immediately after the stretch, the energy is released and it contributes to the total force production capacity of your muscles. Training this elastic ability has shown to effectively improve the production of power and muscle force. This means that if you simply lift weights, you are not taking full advantage of what your body has to offer to help you be more powerful on the field of play.

Setting Up A Workout Plan

Let me give you some basics as to how training affects skill. Generally when you are doing an exercise with weights, a process that is done slowly, you are affecting your muscles the most. If you fatigue the muscles it will typically take two days to recover if you eat and sleep normally. If your training exercises require high speed, or good motor skill control, like medicine ball throws or agility work, you are affecting your nervous system as much, or more than, your muscles. The nervous system is very sensitive and can take three days or more to recover to full function.

Many athletes make the mistake of training by using high skill exercises like lifting weights. They do so much that they get very tired, loosing their ability to perform skillfully, sort of like playing pick-up basketball too long. You just won't move or jump the same as when you were fresh.

Another problem that faces the athlete is lactic acid build-up, or what you would call the *pump* in the weight room. The lactic acid acts like a buffer between your muscles and the nervous system. It can also adversely affect your ability to be crisp and fresh when you need it most. When you are faced with the execution of a technical skill such as throwing a pitch, and you work out the day before on your chest and arms to a point of a big pump, you sort of create a heavy-overcoat effect on yourself. To execute a skill physically your brain talks to the nerves, which then tell your muscles what to do. If you are tired from lifting, the heavy feeling will slow you down and ruin your ability to perform at your best.

As a general guide when working out, if you are performing an exercise requiring speed, don't work to the point of exhaustion where you can't do the exercise with high quality. Always leave room for more. In the weight room, make sure you give yourself enough rest before your next game. During the season you have to stay away from a big pump. Either do heavier weight with fewer repetitions to keep your strength, or use light weights to keep and maintain performance.

With those basic premises in mind, you can now begin to train to throw like an Olympic Champion.

Off-Season Approach

The great part of off-season training is that you don't have to worry about affecting your immediate playing performance. This is the time of year you should be actively pursuing the goal of getting stronger or gaining weight. If you were to try this during the season, there would surely be a loss in your performance, and your chances of injury would increase dramatically.

For maintaining or improving throwing power, you will have to spend a lot of time doing exercises that fall into the strength category of physical training. Exercises done slowly can be done in the off-season because they build strength in the throwing movement. In addition to the strength work, you should continue to do work such as medicine ball throws, but use heavier weighted balls. No matter how much strength work you do, it will be critical for you to maintain some flexibility and range of motion by doing that type of work at least two days a week. All strength work must still be counteracted by work with flexibility and range of motion in mind. As the year progresses, range of motion, flexibility, and speed play more significant roles and should take over as your main focus moving into the pre-season.

Off-season training guidelines:
- Get stronger and gain weight if needed.
- Work two days a week for flexibility and range of motion (medicine ball throws) to maintain throwing skills.
- Use heaviest medicine balls for throwing drills.

Winter And Pre-Season Training

This time of year is when getting fit becomes a reality. Most players will begin running to obtain more cardiovascular fitness so playing games is a lot easier. This is also the time of year you can make a big difference in your ability to throw a ball really hard. You can consider it the period when you close the gap between slow strength training and high speed throwing with a baseball. The game of baseball is a quick game when the ball is in play. Strength training is a slow action. The pre-season training should focus on faster and faster work to get closer to the playing speed of the game. This is why so many players struggle early in the season after heavy weight lifting. Even though they become more powerful, they can't use it in the game because they are not fast enough with the new strength and power they have.

Pre-High School Player Workouts

For athletes not yet in high school, the pre-season is the time they can affect their throwing speed the most. Since I don't advocate weight-lifting for them, their off-season work will probably be spending time playing another sport, but almost every baseball player goes through a bit of a pre-season. Young athletes can train for throwing power by using medicine balls in various weights. Medicine ball throws alone can make a dramatic impact on throwing power to young and non long-term trained athletes.

How Much Training To Do?

Now that you have an idea on what type of training is expected from players to improve their throwing power, how much has to be done?

It is possible to improve your throwing power within 4-6 weeks, with an aggressive training program. The development will depend upon the age and skill of the athlete. Generally pre-high school age athletes show good improvement, but not quite as dramatic as a high-school age athlete. College athletes can still improve very dramatically, but the elite player may find difficulty improving throwing power because he usually has little room for improvement.

Training Days Per Week

Every athlete can benefit from two days a week of medicine ball throwing. It is possible to train 3 days a week if you are an advanced athlete, and for elite players, 4 days a week is common.

Arm Specific Power Drills

Long toss is widely known for improving throwing ability. It is simply playing catch from a great distance. When you practice throwing for distance, the arm develops more power over a period of time. The one concern about long-throwing is the amount of throws you take. The increased pressure on the arm from throwing far requires the players to keep the amount of hard throws within reason to avoid any injuries. Just don't go beyond any feeling of the arm getting tired.

Throwing a ball through the uprights on a football field is another way to test and enhance throwing power. Throwing through the uprights makes the athlete throw accurately and think about throwing through a target. This is one of the key aspects to improve throwing ability which I wrote about earlier in this chapter. You can also measure from how far away you made a field goal with a ball, and test yourself occasionally on your improvement. The best way to test your performance is to take four or five throws from a distance. Move back five yards once you make a good throw, then move back until you miss all your attempts.

Many players use weighted balls to enhance throwing power. It is possible to use heavier and lighter balls than a baseball to work your arm to increase throwing ability. The most important aspect to remember here is that the heavier the ball you throw, the easier you should throw it. Heavy balls should be used to groove the throwing motion. As you use a lighter ball, you can add intensity to the throw. This is a very important point to remember. The reason is the joints that flex during the throwing motion take tremendous pressure from heavy weight, and some people can push beyond the breaking point and really hurt the arm throwing a weighted ball too hard.

The best pattern to use weighted balls is to use progression. Start with the heaviest ball you intend to use, and throw it for two to three weeks. Typically 40 to 60 throws in a workout are what are needed. After three weeks go to a lighter ball and do the same thing. Change weights every three weeks until you get to a lighter ball than the baseball, and you can then throw hard, but use 20 to 40 throws in a workout. You can make a big increase in your ability to throw in just a few months. The best time of year to do this is the pre-season.

The TP Sports Six-Week Power Throwing Workout

The information in this chapter should give you the ability to set up your own training. But if you prefer, I have a plan that will make a dramatic change in your throwing in just 6 weeks. I have taken several exercises, and if you do the training aggressively, it helps almost everybody who tries it. (The training plan is intended for players 12 years old and over and should be done in the pre-season or after the season.)

The Exercises To Do:

Bungee-Resisted Hip Thrusts

Use a rubber cord to resist or hold back your movement. Load the back leg like a pitcher would, and turn and drive the hip like throwing a ball. Just keep your arms at your side and work the hips.

Standing Two Arm Throw

Use two arms over the head and make a throwing motion with the upper body and follow through.

Twist And Throw

Use both arms to take the ball behind the body and then above the head, as you twist to face toward the throw, and fire the ball with both arms.

Multi-Step Throw

Throw the ball with two arms from the overhead position, but use a few steps to increase speed. Sometimes called a crow-hop.

Bungee-Assisted Medicine Ball Throw

Use a rubber cord to pull you into a multi-step throw. The cord will add power to your skill.

Field Goal Throws With Baseball

Try to make a field goal with a baseball. Move back to find your limit.

Weeks One And Two:

Day One

Warm-up

Standing two arm throw 3 x 10 repetitions with 3kg ball

Twist and throw 3 x 10 with 3 kg ball

Multi-step throw 3 x 10 with 2kg ball

Bungee-assisted medicine ball throw 3 x 10 with 1 kg ball

Bungee-resisted hip thrusts 5 x 10

Field goal throws with baseball: Start from a distance you can make on a hard throw easily. Move in 5 yards, then make 5 throws. Start moving back 5 yards every 5 throws until you miss all 5 efforts. Measure the distance, and record it.

Day Two

Same as day one but don't do the field goal throws.

Weeks Three And Four:

Drop the weight of the ball by 1 kg in the standing two-arm throw, twist and throw, and the multi-step throw. Follow the same program as the first two weeks.

Weeks Five And Six:

The weight in all medicine ball throws should now be 1kg. It will feel light for most of you, but you should be very aggressive and throw hard. Follow the same program as the first four weeks.

After you have completed the six weeks, test your throwing ability with the field goal throw, or with a radar device for speed if available.

Conclusion

Training to find more throwing power requires following the guidelines set forth in this chapter. You can use your imagination in coming up with exercises, but stay with basic movements that improve the muscles used in throwing. If you maintain the goal of being a loose, flexible, and powerful athlete, you can become a great thrower. I believe there is someone out there that can throw a 110-MPH fastball, but it will take the proper training and an open mind to get there.

Tom Pukstys

Olympian
Palos Hills, Illinois

U.S. National Javelin Champion, Tom Pukstys, is helping throwers all over the country.

In high school Tom Pukstys played baseball until his junior year when he decided to give track a chance. He joined the track team to throw shot put and discus, and then decided to throw javelin once he reached college. There weren't many experts in javelin throwing at that time, so Tom was self-taught to a great extent. The change in venue from baseball to javelin-throwing paid off during his senior year of college when he set the National American Collegiate Record in the javelin throw and made two Olympic teams, where he became the U.S. National Champion six times. Tom continued to compete internationally for the next eleven years, setting record after record – seven of them American records.

Then in 1996 at age twenty-eight, Tom was invited to try out for the New York Yankees. Although it was nice recognition of his skill and sportsmanship, he decided to continue to focus on track.

Today Tom is a certified strength and conditioning specialist and trains other throwing athletes in the sports of baseball, softball, and football. He has designed his own programs in speed and agility and strength and power to help these athletes gain that important needed edge by throwing harder and improving flexibility and force.

Tom has earned a reputation as a personal trainer, holds seminars on *Throwing Power, Raising Athletic Children*, and *How to Keep an Athletic Household,* and recently developed the *Throw Harder* video. He is often a guest speaker for athletic events, and was recently a speaker at the American Baseball Coaches Association's national convention.

You can reach Tom at: 8361 W. 99th St., Palos Hills, IL 60465; phone: 708-430-4138; e-mail: tpukstys@hotmail.com or TPThrows@worldnet.att.net or through his web-site, www.TPSports.org.

CHAPTER 7

Speed Training For Baseball

Ed Ruisz
Speed Advantage Training

One of the most exciting developments in recent years in baseball training is the inclusion of speed and explosive training to enhance the skills needed to excel in the sport. Specifically the goals of this type of work are as follows:

1) To improve time from the batter's box to first base (a 30-yard sprint). If a player can cut .15 seconds off of this mark, it will cause him to reach the bag over a full yard faster. Just think of how many plays are decided by margins much less than this.

2) To allow a player to steal more bases. Not only is raw speed a vital component of base stealing, but also it is an explosive first step that allows an athlete to accelerate more quickly.

3) To run the bases with better form. This, along with an increase in speed, will allow the offensive team to exert constant

pressure on a defense. This pressure will invariably lead to more opposition errors. It is true that most colleges now ask for a 60-yard test for players (the distance from 1st to 3rd or from 2nd to home). Reducing a 60-yard time by .25 seconds will allow a player to reach the base over two yards faster.

When I work with athletes in the area of speed and explosive training for baseball, I use several pieces of equipment that are reasonably priced. I truly believe that speed-training equipment is to today's athlete what weights have been to players of the last two decades. They represent a significant breakthrough in how major improvements can be made.

The first piece of equipment I use is a Viper, a belt with three D-Rings attached to it – one in the rear and one on each side. You can attach surgical tubing cords or nylon straps (depending on the drill) to the D-Rings. The Viper 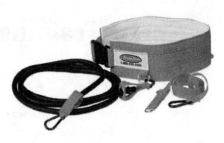 allows for training to be done both resisted and assisted. The Viper costs less than $60 and comes with a belt, one surgical tubing cord, and a nylon resistance strap.

I believe an athlete should purchase a device called the Sidewinder, which has two ankles cuffs attached by a 12-inch piece of thick surgical tubing. The Sidewinder is a superb device for developing leg strength in a variety of drills and is also the equipment of  choice for performing defensive agility drills, which are not the subject of this chapter. We also utilize sprinting parachutes to develop power and speed endurance. These are most helpful in improving the 60-yard dash, too.

Although there are literally dozens of drills that I utilize in training a baseball player, beginners should concentrate on the following categories: a) resisted sprints, b) resisted jumps, c) assisted sprints, and d) base rounding balance drills. These are the areas I would like to cover in this chapter. If you would like any further information or clarification of anything you read, please feel free to call me at (888) 377-3330.

Resisted Sprints

When an athlete sprints at full speed, he is compelled to use a certain amount of his muscle fibers to complete the action. One of the goals of training is to build stronger muscles in the specific range of motion that an athlete uses for sprinting. In this way a player will be able to exert more force off the ground and increase his stride length. One of the best ways to do this is to have an athlete perform his sprints resisted by surgical tubing. This allows the player to use more muscle fibers in the action, and explosive power will be enhanced in much the same way that a weightlifter improves his power (a function of strength times velocity) by overloading his muscles in a weightlifting exercise.

Specific Drill #1: Viper Sprints
Have the athlete run a timed 15-yard sprint without resistance. Then put the viper belt on and clip both ends of the surgical tubing cord out from the back of the belt so that it forms a bow. After making sure the belt is correctly fitted, a partner will grab the bowed end and put tension on the cord standing about 2 ½ to 3 yards behind the runner. On a verbal command, the runner sprints a timed 15-yard sprint with the partner following, still keeping good tension on the tube. The second time should be about 1/3 slower than the first time. For example, a non-resisted sprint of 2.30 should equate to about a 3.00 – 3.10 resisted sprint. If the time is significantly lower than this, the resistance is too little. If the time is higher, (let's say about 3.25) then too much resistance by the partner is being applied. On the second run, adjust accordingly. Very shortly, athletes will begin to understand just how much resistance to apply. If there is too little, the strength gains are too minimal. If there is too much, the speed is slowed to the degree that power gains will be insignificant. As far as

the number of times an athlete should do this drill, I like four resisted reps followed by two non-resisted reps. The first sprint does not count.

Specific Drill #2: Let-Goes

For this drill use the short strap that comes in the Viper package. Have a partner hook it out the back of the belt. On the *Go* command,

the athlete sprints 15 yards at full speed. At that point the partner lets go of the nylon strap and the athlete continues to sprint for another 15 yards to the finish of the drill. The key is to keep the effort the same the entire 30 yards of the sprint. Once again as in drill #1, the resistance should be moderate. The concept of the drill is that the athlete will have his muscle fibers fire at an increased rate, and then when the resistance disappears, the athlete will continue to sprint at the enhanced firing rate, improving acceleration.

Specific Drill #3: Parachute Runs

With younger players (under 14), I believe parachute runs are an excellent choice for resisted running. Since the amount of resistance is not great, a younger athlete will not have a great problem in keeping his running form normal throughout the length of the drill (perhaps 40-60 yards). Parachutes can also be used with older players as part of a training program, but no more than one time per week and over distances of no

less than 60 yards. At the end of the chapter a workout program will be shown. It is also imperative to follow any parachute-resisted runs with non-resisted sprints. This allows the body to incorporate *muscle memory* into the drills as it *remembers* the process by which the body recruits more muscle fibers when running with the parachute.

Resisted Jumps Contrasted With Normal Jumps

All too often baseball players ignore jump training as part of a workout. Each year in Indianapolis, the NFL tests two jumps as part of its battery of drills: The Vertical Leap and Standing Broad Jump. The league does this because both tests reveal an athlete's explosive capabilities and first-step quickness. There is a huge difference between a 300-lb. offensive tackle with a 16" vertical (with luck clearing the height of the *Sunday New York Times*) and one with a 32" leap. The latter player will always be more explosive, athletic, and quicker. The same holds true when one formulates a program to develop baseball speed. If performance can be improved in jump tests, those skills will translate to a quicker first step when stealing bases and more powerful acceleration when coming out of the batter's box and when running the bases. Here are some of the core drills a player should perform.

Specific Drill #4: Vertical Jumps Without Resistance

In this drill an athlete will place his feet armpit-width apart with the toes pointing straight ahead. The athlete should then bend at the knees and sink to a three-quarter squat position. The arms should be behind the body, coiled and ready to spring. On a verbal command by a coach, the athlete leaps upward using both arms to provide momentum and power. The legs should straighten and the athlete should try to have his hands grab an imaginary basketball rebound or football pass over his head. Younger athletes often have a tendency to jump *out*, rather than *up* on the drill, and it is important to tell them to land in the same place that they began the jump.

Specific Drill #5: Vertical Jumps With Resistance

The athlete should now put the orange Viper belt on and hook two rubber tubes (one on each side) in bowed fashion to the D-Rings on the side of the belt. He will need two partners to stand on the tubes (one on each side) halfway up the tube about 12 inches from the outside of the athlete's foot. Each *helper* should firmly hold the

bowed end of the tube. Once the athlete is in place, he should execute 4-6 vertical jumps on the command of his coach or partner. The jumps should be spaced out about every 3 seconds so the athlete can reset his position. Immediately after the resisted jumps, the athlete should remove the belt and perform 4-6 jumps without resistance. Over the course of several weeks this method will definitely increase an athlete's vertical leap and the amount of power he can generate from the joints of the ankles knees and hips.

Specific Drill #6: Multiple Vertical Jumps

This drill is a variation of Drill #5. In this drill the athlete immediately executes vertical jumps each time he hits the ground from the previous jump. The coach or partner does not give a verbal command on each jump but rather says *Go*, and then ten seconds later yells *Stop*. Once again, after doing the drill with the belt and tubing, the athlete should perform the drill without resistance for an equal amount of time.

Assisted Sprints

Over 30 years ago famed Soviet sprint coach, Yuri Versoshansky, did a number of studies where he artificially increased the sprinting speeds of his athletes (either by towing with a car or downhill running on hills with gradual three to five degree slopes), and discovered that in competition his athletes greatly improved their times. Since Versoshanky's initial research, a number of programs based on his findings have been constructed. Here are two of the best drills.

Specific Drill #7: Downhill Sprinting

The athlete should find a slope of about three to five degrees – something so gradual it is not easily noticeable on first glance. The athlete will then run full speed down the hill for about 50 yards with perfect form (discussed later). After completing each sprint, the athlete should rest several minutes and sprint a 40-60 yard sprint over flat ground. Anywhere between 3-5 downhills and 3-5 normal sprints should be done in a workout for young players.

Specific Drill #8: Surgical Tubing Tows

This drill should be done with caution and under the supervision of a coach. Two boys will wear the Viper Belt and connect a tube from the D-Ring of one of the boy's bellies to the other player's back D-Ring. They then should  stand 5 yards apart to stretch the tube. The coach will yell the word, *Go*, whereupon the first athlete sprints out at full speed. One second later (no more than that) the coach says, *Go* a second time and the towed runner begins to sprint. The tow should go about 25 yards. It is always wise for the first tow to be done with the lead runner going out at about 80% so the trail runner can get used to the higher rate of speed. Immediately after each repetition, the towed athlete should do a full speed sprint of about 40 yards. As with downhill running, the total amount of sprints should be in the 3-5 area.

Base Rounding Drills

At Speed Advantage Training, we have worked to improve the ability of players to round the bases efficiently without losing a great amount of speed. No matter what, some speed is lost when rounding. Here are two drills that we feel work especially well.

Specific Drill #9: Circle Runs

Create a circle with cones about the size of the mid-court circle

 on a basketball court (or use the court if possible). Have the athlete run sprints counterclockwise around the circle emphasizing several things: a) dipping the inside shoulder to the center of the circle, b) putting the majority of weight on the outside leg, and c) constantly moving the arms in a sprinting fashion. Each repetition should be three revolutions around the circle. Players should also do one clockwise run for every two counterclockwise runs so that muscle strength will not be developed in an unbalanced manner. A total of 6 circle runs can be completed in a workout.

Specific Drill #10: Lunge Walks With The Sidewinders

If you have a Sidewinder, attach the cuffs to the ankles and perform three 20-yard lunge walks with resistance and one without. The Sidewinder is fantastic for developing muscle strength and flexibility in the same range of motion as a sprint. Other variations of the drill can be butt-kicks, reverse-lunge walks, and lateral shuffles.

Form

It is vital that the young baseball player does not assume that his sprinting form is correct. Using a video camera and slow-motion replay to determine faults, the following points should be examined.

- a) Sprint on the balls of the feet not landing flat-footed or heel first.
- b) After touching down with the ball of the foot, the foot should push back and the heel should come up high towards the buttocks as it completes its stride revolution.
- c) Arms should lock in at a 90-degree angle to allow full shoulder rotation.
- d) The hands should have a range of motion from the back pocket of the athlete's pants to his chin as he sprints.
- e) The palms of the hands should be parallel as the athlete runs.

If they are at angles to each other (usually turned in), the athlete will twist his upper torso.

As in any skill on the baseball diamond, good sprinting form should be practiced and video taped periodically. Athletes who wish to have their form evaluated can send tapes and $30 to Ed Ruisz, 3052 Funks Mill Road, Riegelsville, PA 18077-9712.

The Workout Itself

In a chapter such as this it is difficult to provide all the different types of workouts that a baseball player can do. I have selected an excellent starter package of drills using speed equipment that can be obtained for about $120 through Speed Advantage Training, Inc. When mapping out a workout schedule, I would follow these guide-lines:

a) Train for speed two days per week (three is too much) and devote 30-40 minutes to it.
b) Checking the four categories of drills that I have listed (resisted sprints, resisted jumps, assisted sprints and base-rounding drills), select one drill from each category per workout (four overall). That will allow for about 10 minutes per drill, more than enough time to complete an effective workout.
c) Make sure that all safety regulations are followed when using equipment, and be sure to monitor and treat any muscle pulls or strains. Remember, too much sprinting will not make you faster, it can actually slow you down.

I believe by devoting at least some portion of a player's training to speed, explosion, and acceleration improvement, an athlete will become far more valuable to the team and enhance his skills greatly. Please feel free to call me at any time for further information on training routines or to order equipment.

Ed Ruisz

President
Ed Ruisz's Speed Advantage Training

Ed Ruisz, the president of Ed Ruisz's Speed Advantage Training, has been working on speed development with athletes for over a quarter century. Twice named Pennsylvania Track and Field Coach of the year, Ruisz did graduate work in the former Soviet Union in the areas of speed and power development. He develops specific programs for a number of sports, and has trained athletes from young sports all the way up to the NFL, major college programs and Olympic performers. Ruisz and Vice-President Deron Braswell personally work with almost 2,000 athletes a year through their team training, private training and clinic programs.

You can reach Ed at 888-377-3330 or e-mail him at edru@bel-latlantic.net.

Editors Note: *If you are located near a Frappier Acceleration Clinic (see their ad in the back of the book) and can afford their program, I have found them to be very successful at improving foot speed.*

CHAPTER 8

How To Improve Bat Speed

Karl Schilling
Winning Edge Foundation

In a recent issue of *Baseball Digest* Ted Williams was quoted as saying, *"Bat speed produces power."* One of the greatest hitters in the history of baseball understood the importance of bat speed, but do you?

Bat speed is the single most important measure of how well you swing the bat. Although you need strength to exert bat speed, it is the speed with which the bat head makes square contact with the ball that determines the *power* of your swing. The faster your bat speed, the farther you hit the ball. And when you generate improved bat speed with a heavier bat (increased load), you will *greatly* improve your power.

The MPH Training program that you will learn about in this chapter, was designed to help you maximize your swing power. This training is designed to help you develop a faster bat while swinging a heavier load, and also to develop maximum bat control. These are the tools you need to become a truly great hitter. Although these tools do not automatically make you a great hitter, they will give you the physical components that will help you most in your quest for hitting greatness.

So let's get started. Are you skilled or talented? It is vitally important that you know the difference. Talent abounds, in fact everyone has it, maybe not baseball talent, but talent in some form. For our purposes it is only baseball talent that we will deal with. There are many talented players of all ages, however there are not as many skilled players. There is a major difference between talent and skills. Let's look at these differences.

At a young age baseball players acquire many habits. Unfortunately, due to lack of knowledge (something you will not suffer from after reading this chapter) and improper coaching, the majority of these habits are *bad habits*.

> *NOTE:* **Habit equals**
> **Observation, Repetition, and Internalization.**

There is an age-old adage that states, "Practice makes perfect." The simple truth is: *Practice Makes Permanent!* Most coaches from youth ball through high school practice the basic skills of baseball. This in itself is positive; however, the major mistake made is in the definition of basic skills. The majority of coaches include pitching and hitting in their definition of basic skills. Starting with this premise young players are doomed to having under-developed skills.

The basic skills of the game of baseball are running, throwing and fielding. The advanced skills are pitching and hitting, and should be taught as such. These advanced skills require training and practice, and this is where the major difference can be made in a player's development. Skills are acquired; they are not a birthright.

The best analogy I can make is in the case of a diamond. In its natural state (represents talent) the diamond is a crusty, dirty rock which appears to be of no particular value. In fact, chances are that you would dismiss it and throw it away. However, when it is processed (developed) it is molded into a thing of exquisite beauty and great value. The diamond cutter (coach) is the person who has most of the responsibility in developing the quality and skill of the diamond (player). This is comparable to all ages of baseball players, including young professional players. Many are talented, but until their skills are developed, they cannot maximize their abilities. It is, therefore, imperative that coaches understand skill development techniques and training methodologies. Too many young players have mechanical flaws that will inhibit them from playing this great game at higher levels – college and professionally. These mechanical flaws have developed from a consistent approach of practicing incorrect techniques. This is a marriage of a lack of knowledge combined with poor repetitions.

You avoid this potential pitfall by understanding that there are three ingredients to success:

1) Inspiration to action (action-motivation)
2) Know-How (proper training)
3) Activity knowledge

All success begins with action. You must take some form of action; however, before you do this, it would be advisable to have knowledge or know-how. This knowledge should be general and specific. So a first step to skill development is knowledge. You must know everything about the skills before you can master them. In the case of hitting and pitching, which should be qualified as advanced skills, there are three major areas:

1) Mental Conditioning
2) Mechanics (Swing or Throwing)
3) Physical Conditioning

These are the three components that form an advanced skill. A successful coach must become well versed in the knowledge of these areas. You must begin to understand the differences between training and practice. Whether you are a player or a parent of a player reading this, it is this distinction that will become the key to future success. Once you have made this assessment, it is then, and only then, that you can commit to developing skills. This commitment will be to the training and development of proper skill sets through sound funda-mentals and proper repetitions.

Prior to the improvement of bat speed it is essential that you become mechanically sound in your swing mechanics. There is obviously some bat speed improvement in mechanical improvement. So let us begin at the mechanical stage. As previously mentioned, mental conditioning is one of the three components of the advanced skill. Now what does this have to do with mechanics? Good question! It has everything to do with mechanics.

Mechanics are predicated upon movement, and movement begins in your mind. When we choose to move, the conscious brain using a collection of learned movements (muscle memory) controls the action. For the movement to progress successfully, the brain requires feedback (information that tells the shape of the body, the speed of movement and direction of its actions). This information is provided by the senses of sight (visual feedback), sound (audio feedback), touch and feelings from muscles, joints and balance (kinesthetic feedback). The brain then uses the feedback to determine any appropriate corrective action based on the learned movement. In short what this means is that your swing mechanics begin with your thought process. This is why mental conditioning is so important.

There are three stages to learning a new skill:
1) Identifying and developing of the component parts of the skill.
2) Linking the component parts into a smooth action.
3) Developing the learned skill so that it becomes automatic (internalization).

The learning of physical skills requires the relevant movements to be assembled component by component, using feedback to shape and polish them into a smooth action. Rehearsal of the skill must be done regularly and correctly. I hear you saying, "What does this have to do with me?" In order to correct a mechanical flaw you must relearn the skill. That's right, relearn what you have initially learned incorrectly, which is not as difficult as it sounds. I will give you a training formula to change any mechanical flaw in your swing or other mechanical sets. Pay close attention and do this work before any other training to increase bat speed.

I want you to understand a few simple concepts. We think in pictures. If you need proof, try this: *Pink Elephant*. What happened? Did you get a picture or did you just see words? The picture was probably vivid. This is how your mind works. Your thoughts are transferred to vivid images, which then lead to activity. So in order to change a movement you must first change the image of the movement. This works for all processes by the way. This can be used for academic improvement as well as athletic improvement.

Let's look at a process or formula to enhance your swing mechanics.

1. Identify the mechanical flaw.
2. Describe the new mechanical movement.
3. Have player describe back the new mechanical movement.
4. Drill by the use of proper repetition.
5. Video-tape player doing the new mechanical movement.
6. Have player view video and describe what they are watching.
7. Drill by use of proper repetition.

Notice the use of description in this process. This is based upon the *Law of Effect* that states, "You get more of what you reinforce." Generally what you respond to, you reinforce. So you reinforce your contact with, and awareness of, whatever it is you are responding to. And you are reinforcing whatever skills and traits you are drawing upon for that situation. What I want you to understand is that the more you can find to reward, or even excite your senses and imagination in any body of learning, the more *that* learning is reinforced into full focus of conscious awareness and of immediately retrievable memory. In this case muscle memory or the integration of your swing mechanics to an unconscious event (Habit). What I want you to learn are ways to find your own reinforcements in what you are learning. This will help you learn it more effectively and efficiently.

This part of mental conditioning always seems complex, but it really isn't. It has been my success to relay these concepts to players in easily understandable methods. I don't want you to become a brain scientist, but I do believe that you must have some understanding of the mind process so you can form a belief system and use it in your training.

Every serious researcher of the brain and mind has come to agreement on this point: For every awareness you are consciously experiencing, there are hundreds, if not thousands, of other awarenesses that you are unconsciously experiencing. So how do you use this? By choosing where you want the *Law of Effect* to affect you. In this case it is mechanical improvement; later it will be in ballistic improvement, and having it interact more with what you are seeking to learn (new enhanced mechanical movements).

We develop awareness not only by paying attention to it, but also by responding to it some way and therefore, reinforcing it. (First changing the mental picture of movement and then physically responding to the new movement).

One of the most detailed ways to respond to and reinforce a perception is to describe it in the most detail that you can. You should describe it out loud, to an audience. In this case to a coach or parent.

The next concept is to increase your neurological contact with what you are trying to learn. In other words, visualize the movement in your mind's eye. Get more senses involved; focus on vision, sound, smell, and touch. The more contacts you create, the sooner you will create a new enhanced neuro path. There are thousands of ways to strengthen your neurological contact, the contact of your brain, mind and nervous system, with stuff you are trying to learn. So don't be too surprised at the fact that there are techniques available to you, which if you knew and practiced them, would enable you to create genius level performance. Many think genius exists only in academics. Not true. It exists in all levels of performance. Athletic achievement is based upon genius level performance. You are learning how to become a baseball genius!

You are learning to develop your skills. Understand that all learning is the creative act of the learner. It is not the transfer of information or any other definitions you have been taught. All learning is the creative act of the learner. You are the best teacher of how to improve your skills. Certainly you need reference points, that's what trainers are for, but your training and development is best devised in your own mind and creativity. So what makes for good creating also makes for good learning, and what makes for good learning makes for good creating. This brings us back to the descriptive process. That which you express is 10 to 100 times more productive to your learning than what is expressed to you. Learning is most effective when it is in the form of feedback from one's own activities.

The feedback you receive from proper repetition and proper thought process is the most effective tool you have to developing your skill level. How can you assess your performance? As we discussed in Step 5, use a video camera to record your new movement. This is because initially we compare visual feedback from the athlete's movement with the technical model to be achieved. Athletes should be encouraged to evaluate their own performance. In assessing performance of an athlete consider the following points:

- ◆ Are the basics correct?
- ◆ Is the direction of the movement correct?
- ◆ Is the rhythm correct?

Younger players, or a player who has a major mechanical flaw, should watch videos of big league players and create visual pictures and description of the movements displayed by these highly competent players. This will initiate some major movement improvements. Then players can get specific with their own individual mechanics.

The next process in mechanics is to understand the principles of balance, coordination and strength. It must all begin with balance. Players develop the beginnings of balance from ages 3-7; from 7-12 they acquire coordination, and from 13-25 strength. Of course these can be combined at any age, and the younger the better for obvious neurological purposes. In MPH Training, I learned that to improve balance you should train in slow motion. The slowest movement possible, at which time you will notice the impact on balance. This means practicing your mechanics in slow motion. This will improve both your upper and lower body balance. By linking these movements you can greatly improve coordination, but most coordination comes in the form of reactions.

To improve your reactions you need to train at a high rate of speed. This means to practice your skill at a speed much greater than that which you face in the game. In other words facing pitches from a very close distance at a very great speed. Do not be concerned with swinging and missing as in the beginning you will find it very difficult to make contact. This does not mean you have poor hand/eye coordination, it simply means you are not adjusted to the reaction necessary to be successful. As you continue with this training you will see great results and improvement in your reactions. Soon no speed will be too quick to beat you. This adjustment will not only form an improvement in coordination, but it will also form a visual improvement. When you first face a 90-MPH pitch or faster, you notice it is difficult to see clearly. This is the first level of improvement necessary. You must slow the pitch down visually. This is a learned and acquired skill. If you train at increased speeds, you will acquire this skill and improve reactions.

Slow motion training will improve balance (and strength to some degree), and high-speed training will improve coordination and vision. Regarding strength, it is wise to incorporate different forms of resistance training to improve muscularity and develop improved strength. In baseball this can come in many forms, most obviously weight training, but it can also be incorporated in hitting weighted balls and taking swings against forms of resistance.

Hopefully you now have a picture of the type of knowledge necessary to achieve skill development. I also hope that you have some better understanding of what the differences are between talent and skills. By gaining an understanding of mental conditioning you can vastly improve your physical skills. Everything you do as an athlete is dependent upon your mental improvement. Strengthen the mind, and the body will follow. This is what will separate you from your competition. You will be synergistically based and your competition will be relying solely upon their physical abilities. Your mental capacity will determine your ability to use your physical attributes and skills. There is your difference between talent and skill, talent is physical and skill is mental and physical.

As we begin our discussion on bat speed, I would like to give credit to Paul Nyman of SETPRO, a true pioneer in his field. It was Paul's initial work in the field of bat speed that caught my interest over five years ago. Much of the work I have done has been from the initial research of Paul's. The best equipment for the improvement and measurement of bat speed has been the SETPRO equipment. As we have discussed, hitting is an advanced skill. To improve your hitting requires knowledge about how to improve your swing, some of which we have already discussed. It also requires that you put effort into repetitions of exercises designed to improve your mechanics while increasing your muscle strength and speed. This is what the MPH Training program is designed to do for you.

The key to unlocking the secrets to the advanced skill of hitting lies in the three major elements of the MPH Training program: swing Mechanics, Physical conditioning, and Hitting mentals. We used the acronym MPH to emphasize the fact that swing speed is what is most important to develop.

Swinging a bat is a very complex activity. Hitting a pitched ball involves many muscles, and exerts tremendous stress on vision, brain, and muscle systems. Each of the systems must work together. As you see the ball your brain must make a decision to complete the swing *(Swing)* or stop the swing *(Take)*. The swing begins with the muscles in the lower body and upper body working together in what must be a coordinated and synchronized movement. Some muscles stretch while others contract. This sequence of muscle actions and body movements is called the Kinetic chain. MPH Training is based around this kinetic chain, which was introduced by Paul Nyman of SETPRO.

We must first understand how muscles work. Muscle is made up of fibers (like thin threads). Sensory nerves in the spine to the brain connect groups or bundles of fibers. The combination of bundles, nerves and brain cells are called motor units. When a muscle contracts, only those motor units needed are used and exercised. This is called the principle of specificity.

There are two types of muscle fiber: fast twitch and slow twitch. There are technically also some undefined fibers that have not been activated as fast twitch or slow twitch. Slow fibers take longer to develop strength (contract) than fast fibers. Both exist, side by side, in all of our muscles. The body always tries to use slow fibers, because these fibers use less energy than fast twitch fibers. Our bodies are always trying to use the least amount of energy necessary to complete a task. This is a survival instinct, but the advanced skill of hitting requires the use of fast twitch fibers as well, since power is both strength and speed combined together.

To get the body to use its fast twitch fibers, we target them by overloading the body. By swinging hard and as fast as you can, you force the body to use fast twitch fibers. The more fast fibers you can get to contract and use their energy, the more effective your training. In addition you must continually vary your training loads, because if you don't, the body quickly adapts and your progress comes to a screeching halt. This is where many programs have been poorly designed. You will find many programs that promote overload training (heavy bats) or underload training (light bats), and while either of these systems will show initial improvement, in the long run they will create a severe strength or speed deficiency. This deficiency is due to the concept of adaptation.

MPH Training uses heavy loads with explosive workouts in the correct variations to obtain maximum fast fiber activation. Similarly we work out other muscle groups for speed by purposefully underloading in many of the training exercises. To properly train like this you must think in terms of step climbing. As you climb there comes a leveling off period where in order to continue to climb, your body needs to identify strength or speed. We borrowed this concept from the Russians and Eastern Europeans who have used these principles acquired successfully over the years in training their Olympic athletes.

MPH Training includes ballistic training. Swinging a bat requires muscle acceleration through the entire range of motion. This is why most coaches stress following through. Exercises that allow the muscles to accelerate all the way through a range of motion are called ballistic exercises. Remember that the body always tries to protect itself and does only what it has to. Whenever you move an arm or leg, only those muscle fibers that are really needed are used. Every motion then uses different sets of motor units.

Most hitters have a large number of motor units that have never been used because they simply *do not swing enough.* Many are lucky to get 20 batting practice swings 3 times a week. Or, if they take more swings, they usually are not the right kind of swings. The average professional player takes approximately 300 hundred swings a day, sometimes even more in their first two years. If you do not take enough of the right kind of swings, you do not use all the muscle fibers (motor units). Getting all of you muscle fibers to work exactly as you wish, when you want them to, by exercising through the correct range of motion, is called *neural recruitment.* It has been my experience that most ballplayers can improve neural recruitment and thus improve bat speed. In fact when you increase strength through weight lifting, you gain muscle fiber, which means fresh non-recruited motor units. This is great news because it means you can continue to increase bat speed through neural recruitment.

Neural recruitment is the way to gain large amounts of power in a very short period of time. I have personally seen players increase as much as 25 MPH in 30 - 45 days. This training shows you how to overload the correct muscles and motor units required to increase your swing strength and speed *(Power).* We do this with swing exercises. Personal trainers talk about transfer; a real key to efficient sports training. Exercises with little or no relation to the skill being developed have no transfer. Exercises that can most closely duplicate the hitting motion and speed of swinging will best train the muscle fibers used in the advanced skill of hitting. MPH Training is sports-specific training for hitters wanting to develop a powerful swing. You want your training to maximize every swing and make your fast muscle fiber available instantly for maximum power.

Here is what most programs look like:
- ◆ Weight Training
- ◆ (Missing Links)
- ◆ Practice

At Winning Edge we developed MPH Training to use the SETPRO Model of Kinesthetic link as follows:
- ◆ Strength Training
- ◆ Power Conversion
- ◆ Swing Load Training
- ◆ Reaction Stress Training
- ◆ Practice

Strength training is not simply lifting weights. The biggest misconception regarding weight training is that sometimes you gain too much muscle mass, which results in a lack of flexibility. Obviously this can inhibit development of swing power, which requires speed plus strength. Gaining muscle mass early is positive, as it comes with new motor units for neural recruitment. A properly devised weight program for baseball emphasizes low repetitions and some high loads. Fast twitch muscle fibers require heavy loads before they kick in. Flexibility is a most important component in the properly designed program.

One of the better programs I have seen used the concept of ballistic training with weight training to improve balance and strength. This program has yielded great results. All players require some form of resistance training to reach their maximum power. These exercises are Range Of Motion (ROM) exercises that develop and maintain flexibility and endurance while building strength. ROM exercises use the largest different number of motor units and muscle groups, and develop good muscle balance. ROM exercises are performed with body resistance exercises (push-ups, crunches, dips, pull ups, chin ups, etc.), dumb bells, or resistance tubing. Not doing these exercises can create muscle imbalance (a major cause of injury) and restricted movement (muscle-bound effect). Also be aware that the mental concepts we discussed earlier can also be used in your strength training.

Power conversion involves taking the strength you have developed from your strength work outs and training it into the right muscle groups through ROM exercises specific to the skill being developed, in this case swinging a bat. Some of the exercises involved in MPH Training are designed to develop proper swing mechanics, while going through the desired range of motion. Other exercises work to train the proper muscle responses while practicing the exact swing motion to be duplicated while hitting a ball. It is important to note that a number of studies show that simply *wanting* to swing hard is very important in developing muscle speed.

SETPRO has completed a study where two groups of college baseball players were used. For 8 weeks, the two groups did identical swing training, except that group 1 did not have immediate feedback on the speed of their swings while group 2 did. Group 2 was motivated with every swing to swing as hard as possible by the measurement feedback they received, and because of that, group 2 averaged 6 MPH more improvement in their swing speeds over the study period. This is a tremendous difference at the college level.

The program you develop needs to provide you with a roadmap of swing exercises to perform that employ the concepts of ballistic overload training, neural recruitment, and transfer to maximize your swing power. This is what I have done for several hundred players. Remember, strength alone is not power. Speed alone is not power. Speed with strength is real power. Driving the baseball requires power (fast strength). You can be very strong, but if that strength is slow strength, your ability to develop power is very limited. MPH swing load training is designed to help you develop *power* by working the right groups of muscles in the right amounts so that you will develop *fast strength.*

Another important concept is that of *periodization*, which refers to how often you do the exercises. Too much training and you are over trained and fail to improve. Too little and you will not reach your maximum capability. The MPH Training program answers these questions for you so that you can train according to a plan. Our consulting service and toll free line offer you the ability to call in and have me customize the workout even more to your particular needs if necessary.

Reaction Stress Training

Hitting a baseball is the most difficult event in all of sports. It requires the combination of eyes, brain, nerves and muscles working together in rapid and powerful neural path teamwork. An error of one-tenth of a second is the difference between success and failure. Hitting a baseball is also a reaction event. Once the decision is made to swing, everything becomes a reaction. There is no time to consciously think about hands, hips, arms, rotation, extension, etc. Everything will perform as it has been programmed to in advance. And the only way to develop good programming is by hours, months and years of practice swinging a bat.

But there are two kinds of bat speed: Practice speed and Game speed. Practice bat speed is the raw maximum bat speed you can generate hitting off a tee or taking a dry cut. Game bat speed is bat speed under the stress of hitting a pitched ball. The difference between the two can be as much as 10-15 MPH, which translates into 50-70 feet in distance. Hitting off tees and soft toss are important, but they do not adequately exercise and develop the eye-brain-muscle connection. Hitting off a pitching machine does not simulate the wind-up pitch timing for maximum swing rhythm. If you are a serious student of baseball, I highly recommend that you train against the SETPRO reaction Training System. This device was designed to simulate a pitched ball, and can simultaneously measure both your swing speed and the accuracy of your timing to a simulated pitch. If you do not have this equipment to train against, I recommend you swing under stress against a machine set to pitch somewhat faster than the fastest pitch you would see at your level of competition. This builds muscle patterns that enable your faster reaction time. As a hitter this will allow you to wait on the ball longer, have greater command of the strike zone (drive zone), and maintain maximum bat control with power to drive the ball.

The last part of MPH Training is called *hitting mentals*. All great hitters have an edge in addition to their physical skills. They are mentally tough! We can teach you what you need to know to be tough at the plate in each at bat. This involves training in several areas including:
   ◆ Having a belief system
   ◆ Having a proper approach to hitting
   ◆ Hitting philosophy
   ◆ Relaxation

- Visualization
- Concentration
- Pitch identification
- Drive zone recognition
- Plate coverage
- The 2 strike philosophy
- Situational hitting
- The slump buster

Diligence in applying these mental lessons can be as beneficial to your hitting effectiveness as is the increase in bat speed that you are sure to see. Hitting Mentals rounds out the MPH Training program into a holistic approach that lets you learn what the pros know.

This program has worked with players at all levels of baseball, and the results have been proven time and again. Our clients have vastly improved strength, speed, and reaction time. This results in more *power* and greater hitting performance.

Hopefully this has answered many questions for you and challenged you to ask some more questions. Your development as a player requires desire, determination, dedication and discipline. These are the principles that will drive you toward your goals, dreams and aspirations. My greatest hope is that the information provided here motivates you to take action – the action necessary for you to become the skilled player you desire to be. Nothing can happen until you take some action. Action leads to results. Sometimes those results are in the form of failure, but that is a good thing. Failure is your greatest teacher. It will develop the lessons you need to learn in order to make adjustments. So do not be afraid to fail. Act as though it were impossible to fail! As you start to improve you will gain confidence, and this confidence will propel you on to even greater achievements. So get started today, believe in yourself, be willing to take a risk (the potential of failure), take action, review the results and make adjustments where necessary.

This is a winning formula: Work Hard Today, As Dreams Do Come True!

Karl Schilling

Winning Edge Foundation

For the past 30 years, Karl Schilling has been involved in the great game of baseball at the professional, international, college and high school levels. This journey has seen him wear the hats of player, coach, personal instructor, trainer and scout. This experience has included evaluating talent, developing talent and assisting players through the maze of advice and information. His player development resume posts over 49 players who have been selected in the Major League Draft, which also includes his son. During the past two drafts he has personally consulted with 25 players.

The purpose of developing *The Winning Edge* was to compile the very best information available, covering such areas as: skill development, training techniques, physical conditioning, mechanics, mental conditioning, preventative sports medicine and updates on training tools, devices, instructional books, tapes and videos.

For more on Coach Schilling and his programs go to http://winningedgefoundation.com , call 1-888-521-6615 or e-mail him at pzzone@aol.com.

CHAPTER 9

How To Become A
Complete Hitter

Dave Hudgens
Author of *Hitting for Excellence*

One of the most important things a hitter can teach himself is how to be a complete hitter. Part of being a complete hitter is being able to hit the ball to all parts of the field. This is vitally important to a hitter because when you are able to do this:

* The pitcher is not able to pitch to you in any one particular way. In other words, he will have to work much harder to keep you off the bases.
* The defense cannot shade you to one particular area of the field.

If you watched the 2002 World Series, you may have noticed how the Anaheim Angels' defense was playing Barry Bonds. The defense shifted to the right side of the field, except for the third baseman, Troy Glaus, who moved to the shortstop position. This left most of the left side of the infield open. The reasons they did this were 1) Barry is strictly a pull hitter, and 2) the Angels were trying to get him out by pitching him on the inside part of the plate. This is the problem with a pull hitter. They can easily be defensed. Barry is basically a pull hitter, but he, and every pull hitter (even as outstanding as Barry is), will have much more success when they learn how to use the whole field.

When I look back on my playing career, I realize that I was a pull hitter because I had quite a bit of power. This means that being a left-handed hitter, I hit the ball to right field quite often. So consequently, I made a living off hitting ground ball outs to second base on the outside pitch. I did not learn until later in my career that there was something called left field. If I had learned this earlier in my career, and learned to hit the outside pitch to the opposite field, I would have been a much more successful hitter.

Let's take a look at the three different areas of the field. The field is divided up into three areas. They are as follows:

- ◆ The pull side
- ◆ The middle
- ◆ The opposite field

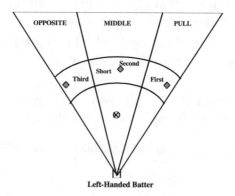

Left-Handed Batter

A left-handed hitter's pull side is from the second baseman to the first base line and out to the outfield fence. The left-handed hitter's opposite field is from the shortstop to the third base line and out to the outfield fence. In between those two areas is the middle.

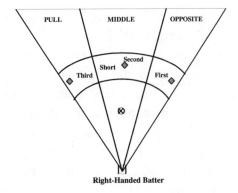

Right-Handed Batter

A right-handed hitter's pull side is from the short stop to the third base line and out to the outfield fence. The right-handed hitter's opposite field is from the second baseman to the first base line and out to the outfield fence. In between those two areas is the middle.

Hitting The Ball To The Opposite Field

To hit the ball to the opposite field you need to:

- ◆ Get a pitch on the outside part of the plate.
- ◆ Hit the ball deeper in the contact zone.
- ◆ Keep the barrel of the bat above your hands.
- ◆ Stay inside the ball.

Most good hitters have the ability to pull the ball. However, to be a complete hitter, you must develop the ability to hit the ball to the opposite field. One reason many hitters have a difficult time hitting the ball to the opposite field is that coaches are always telling them to pull the ball and hit the ball way out front. In order to be able to hit the ball on the outside of the plate, you need to wait until the ball is deeper into the zone. You should try to make contact with the outside pitch when it is even with your front foot or slightly deeper. This is also a good way to handle the curve ball.

Strengths And Weaknesses

The way you stand in the batter's box may show the pitcher where your strengths and weaknesses are. For example, a right-handed hitter that stands off the plate in a closed stance and strides toward the plate is going to handle the ball on the outside part of the plate better than the inside pitch. His weakness would be the inside part of the plate. This is different from a right-handed hitter who has an open stance and stays open on his stride. His strength will be the inside pitch. His weakness will be the ball on the outside part of the plate. This is basically the same for left-handed hitters. This is why I recommend that no matter how you stand at the plate, when your stride foot comes down, you need to be in a parallel stance.

However, as I stated earlier, some hitters have to use the open or closed stance because of flaws in their approach. If you are one of those hitters, make sure you are disciplined enough to swing at the pitches you can handle (your strengths), and do not swing at a ball in your weak area until you have two strikes on you.

Know What Kind Of Hitter You Are

The first step to becoming a complete hitter is to know and understand what type of hitter you are. Are you big and strong – a power hitter? Or are you smaller and maybe a line drive hitter? If you are small and swinging for the fences all the time, you will end up with a lot of medium fly ball outs. On the other hand if you are strong and hit a lot of ground balls, you are not taking advantage of your strength. You should naturally know what type of hitter you are.

Areas Of The Zone

Now that you know the areas of the field, let's examine the area of the zone that you may be pitched to.

- If you are being pitched inside, and you are looking for a pitch inside, you will want to hit this particular pitch to the pull side of the field.
- If you are being pitched right down the middle, you'll want to try and hit this ball up the middle.

- If you are being pitched away, you need to hit to the opposite field.

Many major league hitters will tell you that a key point here is to look for the pitch down the middle. Until you have two strikes on you, you should be prepared to swing and even begin your swing assuming the pitch will be down the middle. You would only hold back from swinging if the ball wasn't in the middle zone. This, of course, is different if you have two strikes on you. At this point you have to be ready to swing at any ball that is close to the plate.

By thinking middle it is much easier to adjust to balls off the middle than it is on the extreme outside or the extreme inside. There will always be times when you need to look for pitches on the inside or outside of the plate. For example, if a pitcher consistently throws to you on the outside of the plate, you need to crowd the plate and look for the ball on the outside part of the plate and then hit the ball to the opposite field. If this is the case, you need to let the pitch on the extreme inside part of the plate go.

If you feel the pitcher is trying to pitch to you outside, then look outside. Do the same with inside. Many pitchers don't have great control, so it is best to always look to the middle. However, good high school pitchers and above (college and pro) do have better control. A key point to remember is that you can look outside and still have a chance to hit the inside pitch, but if you look inside, you will have virtually no chance to hit the outside pitch. This may sound a bit complicated, but all good high school hitters that hope to advance to college or beyond need to learn how to use the entire field and to look for pitches in different areas. The following chart illustrates the areas of the strike zone. Take note where the average player will have his best averages, then find the areas where you hit best.

STRIKE ZONE CHART

.180	.200	.250	.280	.280	.200	.180
.180	.210	.250	.285	.285	.210	.180
.180	.220	.260	.290	.290	.220	.180
.200	.240	.330	.350	.350	.240	.200
.220	.280	.370	.370	.370	.280	.220
.230	.300	.370	.400	.380	.300	.230
.250	.320	.380	.400	.380	.300	.250
.230	.310	.310	.310	.310	.310	.230
.220	.250	.280	.280	.280	.250	.220
.180	.230	.230	230	.230	.230	.180

Situational Hitting

Another important aspect to being a complete hitter is being prepared to hit in specific situations. This is really what sets you apart from being an average hitter to being a very good hitter. A situational hitter has the ability to handle the bat and execute in particular situations when asked to do so. Below are some examples of situational hitting:

- If you are at the plate with a runner on second base and nobody out, you need to advance the runner over to third base with less than two outs. The reason for this is that you want to have a runner on third base with less than two outs so you can score a run on a deep fly ball to the outfield or a ground ball to the infield, which is playing back. You can accomplish this in a number of ways. You can sacrifice the runner over with a bunt. You can hit a grounder to the right side of the infield. You can hit a fly ball to center or right field, hopefully, deep enough to advance the runner. You can get a wild pitch or passed ball or a balk, or you can simply get a base hit. Ideally, you would want to see a pitch middle to outside and not an inside pitch.

- Now that the runner is on third base, we can illustrate another example of situational hitting. If you are at the plate now as a hitter, you would like to try to hit the ball right up the middle, preferably in the air. A ground ball to the right side would also do it. Again, you want to try to take the pitcher as deep into the count as you can. By making a pitcher throw more pitches, you increase the odds of a balk, a wild pitch, a passed ball, being hit by a pitch, a walk or getting a good pitch that you can drive for a hit.

- Another example of situational hitting would be the hit and run. In the hit and run, the base runner starts running when the pitcher starts his delivery to home. The hitter must make contact with the ball. The idea here is to stay out of the double play. The second baseman or shortstop must cover second base, which creates a large hole in the infield at one of those two positions. If the hitter hits the ball through one of the holes, your team will most likely have runners at first and third; however, if the hitter does not make contact, there is a good chance the runner might be thrown out at second base. Usually you would execute a hit and run when the count favored the batter seeing a hitable pitch. This is not something you would do, for instance, when the count is 0-2 on the batter. A hit and run could be a big play for or against your team, depending on if the hitter is able to handle the bat and get the job done.

Selective Hitter

Being a complete hitter is being a selective hitter. As a hitter you need to develop good strike zone knowledge and understand what pitches you can best handle and what pitches you have problems with.

Selectively Aggressive

There is a term that I like to use that is called being *selectively aggressive*. This means understanding which pitches you can really drive. One of the most important things that you can do as a hitter is to get a good pitch to hit. As I've mentioned previously, you want to think *swing* on every pitch until you recognize that it is not in your pre-determined area. Your pre-determined area is the pitch that you have the most success with. This will vary from player to player.

If you are not a selective hitter, pitchers with good control will eat you alive. For example, let's take a look at Greg Maddux, all-star pitcher for the Atlanta Braves. He never gives the hitter a good pitch to hit unless he absolutely has to. There is no reason for a pitcher to give a good pitch to a hitter who does not wait for one. In other words, if Maddux throws a pitch on the outside corner and the hitter swings at it, you can bet the next pitch will be a little bit further outside. Only the most patient hitters will have success off Greg Maddux or control pitchers like him. The key is to be patient and to be selective.

Practice Being A Selective Hitter

A good way to practice being a selective hitter is in live batting practice or when you are doing short toss drills. You can have your coach, parent or a friend call out the count. For example:

- If he calls out 3-1, you would be looking for your pitch in your area because the pitcher now has to throw a good strike. This enables you to look for a pitch in your strong area.
- On the other hand if your coach calls out 0-2, then you must protect the plate and be ready for anything.

The Breaking Ball

There are very few hitters in baseball that can consistently hit a good breaking ball. The best chance that hitters have to hit the breaking ball is when pitchers make mistakes. A mistake is a breaking ball that stays up in the strike zone. The best way to learn to hit a breaking ball is as follows:

- Keep your weight back.
- Keep your front shoulder closed.
- Stay inside the ball.
- Wait for the ball to get deep in the contact zone.
- Hit the ball back through the middle.
- Track the ball with your eyes through all three zones.

Remember that no one hits a great breaking ball, however, no pitcher can consistently throw great breaking balls. If a pitcher makes a mistake, you will be able to make good consistent contact if you follow the above steps.

Pay The Price

Mastering the art of becoming a complete hitter is not something that happens overnight. Hitters in the major leagues still work on this on a daily basis. To become a complete hitter you need to:

- Practice and do your drills faithfully.

- ◆ Take initiative to be a student of the game.
- ◆ Be prepared to think situationally.
- ◆ Recognize hitting situations without being told.

The price you pay in hard work is minimal compared to the benefits you will receive. You will not be a one-dimensional hitter who can easily be pitched to and easily defensed. Your coaches and teammates will have confidence in you to do the job. You will have no weaknesses!

Dave Hudgens

Author: *Hitting for Excellence*
Masterplan Sports and Fitness, Scotsdale, Arizona

From Little League to the Major Leagues, Dave Hudgens has taught hitting to some of the best baseball players in the country. At seventeen Dave was a first-round pick for the New York Mets. He chose instead to accept a full scholarship to Arizona State University. A former *Baseball America All-American,* Dave went on to play in Three College World Series and helped win a national championship.

In his first year in the minors, he hit .298 with twenty-nine home runs. Dave was in his second year of Triple A Ball when injuries forced an end to his playing career. However, the Oakland A's offered him a staff position, and after four years with the A's, Dave accepted the position of hitting coordinator for the Houston Astros. In 1996, Dave went back to the A's as the Assistant Director of Player Development and Hitting Coordinator. In 1999, the A's broke offensive records which had stood for 30 years.

Dave established *Masterplan Sports and Fitness* in 1997 to offer his knowledge of hitting to a wider audience. He saw a real need to correct some of the incorrect information players from Little League to college were getting on hitting. He also found himself dealing with signed professional players who didn't have a clue about the proper way to swing a bat.

Dave is now considered one of the foremost hitting experts in the country. He has an international clientele that he works with through his books and videos. Several of his students have gone on to play Division I and professional baseball.

You can reach Dave at: 480-675-9991 or e-mail him at hitting@hitting.com, or go to his web-site <u>www.hitting.com</u>.

CHAPTER 10

How To Win With Intangibles

Brian Shoop
Head Coach, Birmingham-Southern College

In 2001 Birmingham-Southern was fortunate enough to win the National NAIA Championship. In 2002 we moved to Division I, a decision our administration reached based primarily on the exodus of schools from NAIA and possible future moratoriums. Because of Birmingham-Southern's strong academic reputation, the administration eliminated Division II. Division III was an option, but our strong athletic heritage ultimately pointed to Division I. 2002 proved to be a real challenge for our program as we played some Division I powers in our schedule.

Given the small size of our school (roughly 1500 students), our high standards academically, and our relatively high cost to some other schools, our pool of qualified candidates is somewhat limited. The type of player we attract is usually very smart. Our players aren't perfect and are not saints, but they are a cut above. We have lots of class presidents, national honor society participants, and churchgoers. A young man doesn't necessarily pick us for sports only, but it certainly is a factor. Combine this with the desire to be challenged in the classroom, the small student-faculty ratio, and a strong church-based school that will challenge faith in God, and we end up with a multi-faceted kid who is attracted to us.

Our program looks for a few Josephs of the Bible. (Joseph was above reproach, did everything right, was humble, honest, punished unjustly, but hung in there.) We want kids to be coachable, teachable, hard working, committed to the team, and to the group. We often pray together.

As you can see, to make our program and system work, we are looking for a pretty special kid. Our ballplayers don't have long hair, earrings, or wear hats in the classroom. They have an incredible reputation on campus. Our players are usually the types of guys that parents hope their daughters bring home!

It costs $25,000 to go to Birmingham-Southern. We only have 11.7 scholarships, and with twenty-four on the team, it is important that our players have good academics and can receive an academic scholarship. To get one he will need a good GPA and ACT of 28-29.

The reason I'm giving you all this information is because I feel it is important for you to know that we have special kids. Perhaps these strategies I'll be discussing wouldn't work with kids that don't take instruction well or haven't got the faculties to take it all in and absorb it.

At Birmingham-Southern, we believe that we must win the big inning game. For us, playing for a run at a time will not win games. Ninety percent of all major league wins go to the team with the biggest inning. Fifty percent score more runs in one inning than the other team does in the entire game. I went back and tracked our recent records over the past three years, and when our team scored seven runs or more, we were 109-11. When we scored less than seven runs, we were 38-33, or just an average team. In the big leagues seventy-five percent of all three-plus run innings include a walk, error or hit by pitch. Ninety percent of all five-plus innings include a walk, error or hit by pitch.

How do you win the big inning game? You can win it by hitting home runs, but we are not a power hitting team. You can have a big inning with conservative hits, but the odds of three consecutive hits are 27-1 according to Skip Bertman.

Our team needs to win the freebie war. Last year we kept statistics that proved the success of this method. Let's look at walks. BSC had 342 walks compared to the opposition's 248 walks. We had 87 errors and the opposition had 159 errors. Hit by pitches was pretty close. Pitches hit our players 56 times, and hit our competition 52 times. We stole 128 bases to our competition's 28 stolen bases. If you had to add it all up, we had an extra five free runners per game. This could mean the run differential we need to win the game.

Our team works diligently to be in a position to win the freebie war. How can you as a player help win the freebie war? What can you personally do to pressure your opponent?

You need to be good at the short game. At Birmingham-Southern we have no such thing as a sacrifice bunt. We are always bunting for a base hit. We try to pressure the defense. You can teach yourself bunting just like we do by putting lines on the field. Below you'll find how we set up our field.

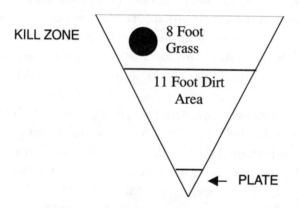

If you look at the circle in the 8-foot grass area, this is our kill zone. In most cases if you put the ball in this spot, it is a base hit. If you place the ball in the 8-foot grass area, you most likely will create a hurried play where the defense will hopefully have to eat the ball or throw it away. At worse case we move the man on first over to second.

How do you put the ball where you want to? To deaden the ball you need to bunt the ball on the tip of the bat, not on the sweet spot. We use a specially designed bat that sculpts out part of the sweet spot and leaves the bat with a large tip. We hold the bat close to the tip with one hand, and we work on this a lot to become proficient at it. We hit ball after ball on this drill. Brett Butler, one of the game's best bunters, once told me he bunted 500 times a day. If you do something 500 times a day, you should get pretty good at it.

The key to making this work is to make sure you practice with adequate bunt velocity. It doesn't do you any good to be practicing this off 40-MPH pitching. Make sure you face a machine throwing at a decent velocity, and make sure you face breaking pitches. Try and make practice conditions as game-like as possible.

You also need to be good at situational hitting. Good situational hitting puts tremendous pressure on the defense. Here's an example: We have a runner on second and no one out. What do we do? The normal thing to do is either try to hit a ground ball to the right side or a fly ball to right to advance the runner. What we like to see is a missile to right field that we score on that is mishandled by the right fielder. That allows our runner to move to second. Your job is to get the right pitch and hit it hard to the opposite field.

The way you get good at this is to practice it. I see a lot of batting practices where players try to crank the ball out of the park on every pitch. You can't learn situational hitting if you don't practice it every day. When you take your cuts, practice hitting some pitches to the opposite field. Learn what to do in various situations: runner on third, one out; runner on second, no one out; winning run on third, man on first, and one out. Learning situations and what to do when you see them will make you a better hitter.

The third component of pressure offense is pressure through the running game.

1) We tell our players to take as big a lead as they can. We want the pitcher to throw to first. We want him to make a lot of throws. We want the pitcher to lose his focus.

2) Unless you are close to 80% successful, you don't have the green light with us. Our normal lead is around 13 feet. Stake it out on the field so you can have an idea of where you should go. Have someone time you. If you can make it to second in

3.4 seconds or less, we will probably give you the green light.

3) Put pressure on the defense by advancing on dirt balls. To do this you have to start your move before the ball hits the dirt. You need to be moving when it does.

4) A runner on first should try to move to third on every base hit. Talk to your coach about aggressive base running. Our program awards risk taking. We don't punish an aggressive base runner. We want our players to be working all the time to put pressure on the defense.

5) Finally, put pressure on the defense through strike zone discipline. If there is anything a pitcher likes, it is a batter who isn't aware of the strike zone. Learn the strike zone and what spots you do best at.

We set up our strike zone as follows:

7	8	9
4	5	6
1	2	3

You need to learn what zones you do well with, and what zones give you trouble. A low-ball hitter will be comfortable swinging for balls in zones 1, 2 and 3, but should stay away from zones 7, 8 and 9. The secret to good hitting is to get your pitch to hit, and not settle for the pitcher's pitch. As a hitter you must be willing to take pitchers deep in the count. This accomplishes two things: 1) It gives you more chances of seeing your pitch, and 2) It wears the pitcher out. If you can knock a team's ace out in the 5th inning instead of the 7th, you increase your odds of winning. Also remember that walks often win games.

In summary if you can make yourself proficient at the little things such as the ones we mentioned, you make yourself a better ballplayer and ultimately give your team a better chance of being victorious.

Brian Shoop

Head Coach
Birmingham-Southern College

The 2003 season marks Brian Shoop's thirteenth year at the helm of the Birmingham-Southern College baseball team. From the time he arrived on campus one of his main objectives was to return the Panthers to the prominence they experienced in the late 1970s and early 1980s. After twelve seasons Brian Shoop has certainly accomplished his goal.

Brian's twelve-year record stands at 487-220-1, and in the past decade the Panthers have captured six regular season conference titles and seven conference tournament championships. The Panthers have made eight regional appearances and finished no worse than third with three runner-up finishes and three regional championships. BSC has been ranked in the final NAIA poll in nine of Brian's eleven years with seven top-ten rankings and three top-five rankings, and 2000 marked the program's seventh consecutive forty-win season.

Brian continues to receive accolades from his peers. He was twice named *TranSouth* Conference *Coach of the Year* and has been honored as the *ABCA Mid-South Region Coach of the Year* three times. He has also been named either *Conference Coach* or *District Coach of the Year* five out of the past eight years and served as the *NAIA Southeast Region Baseball Chairman* for three years. He has been the guest speaker at the *ABCA National Convention* twice, and in 1996, was inducted into the Malone College Athletic Hall of Fame. Following a successful debut in NCAA Division I with over 30 victories, Brian was named 2002's *All-Independent Baseball Team's Coach of the Year.*

Before joining the BSC staff, Brian served as an assistant coach at Mississippi State University. Over a seven-season span (1983-1989) he helped the Bulldogs win three Southeastern Conference Championships and earn six regional appearances and One College World Series appearance. During his Starkville tenure Brian coached Will Clark, Rafael Palmerio, Jeff Brantley, and Bobby Thigpen, and was instrumental in recruiting some of the top players in America.

An Ohio native, Brian began his coaching career at his alma mater, Malone College, where he was an all-district performer. Malone was the Ohio NAIA Champion in each of his six years as a player and coach. He earned a double undergraduate degree (physical education and business/economics) from Malone, and a Masters Degree in sports administration from Kent State University in Ohio. He has also completed his doctoral course work in Educational Leadership at Mississippi State.

Brian and Brenda Shoop have five children: Scott, Emily, Hannah, and twins, Sarah and Jesse.

You can reach Brian Shoop at: bshoop@bsc.edu or at Birmingham-Southern College, 900 Arkadelphia Rd., Birmingham, AL 35254 – Phone: 205-226-4944.

CHAPTER 11

Proper Nutrition:
Fuel For The Ballplayer's Body

Ken Mannie
Strength/Conditioning Coach
Michigan State University

We live in an age that offers a wealth of good nutritional information, while at the same time tickling our ears and tempting our taste buds with fa(s)t food jingles. Call it the palatable paradox.

Adding to the confusion are the ubiquitous diet plans, potions, powders, and magic muscle pills. The result: A murky stew of information, misinformation, and questionable claims.

The challenge for baseball players is to find and implement the nutritional facts. If they don't, it can adversely affect their performance, not to mention their long-term health.

It may not be the most enjoyable part of the job, but coaches must place nutritional education high on their priority list. At Michigan State we have a very basic, sound nutrition program that is qualified with scientific facts, not hearsay, hype, or big name endorsements.

All decisions made on any nutritional component (*i.e.,* training table menu, travel meals, and supplements) are made collectively by the medical, sports medicine, and strength/conditioning staffs. By putting our heads and resources together, we feel that our athletes receive the most up-to-date, safe, sound, and scientifically founded information available.

Our Department of Food, Science and Nutrition is also very active in our program in that they supply interns for consultation, education, and group activities that address the myriad questions, concerns, and misconceptions.

Building A Solid Foundation

The first step in developing a nutritional strategy is to examine the Food Guide Pyramid (Illustration #1). Constructed by the U.S. Department of Agriculture, the Food Guide Pyramid (FGP) presents an ergogenic template for daily food consumption. The six basic nutrient categories (carbohydrate, protein, fat, vitamins, minerals, and water) are proportionally represented in the FGP.

Let's first take a look at what are known as the macronutrients: carbohydrates, protein, and fats.

Illustration #1   *Dept. of Agriculture Food Guide Pyramid*

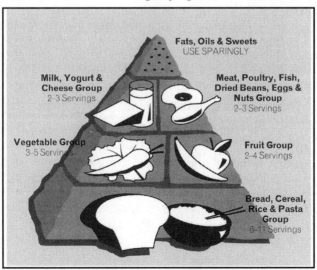

Carbohydrates

Without question, breads, grains, cereals, pasta, fruits, and vegetables should be the basis of an athlete's diet. A carbohydrate-rich diet will keep the muscle and liver glycogen stores, and blood glucose, at optimal levels.

Glycogen is your body's fuel, especially for high-intensity athletic activities. Athlete's who *hit the wall* with fatigue are usually guilty of not ingesting appropriate amounts of carbohydrates. Subsequently their muscle and liver glycogen supplies are too low to fuel the activity.

Athletes should ingest 3-4 grams of carbohydrate per pound of body weight on a daily basis.

Heavy training or practice periods require additional attention. Within 15 minutes of the completion of the session/practice, a carbohydrate-rich food or drink should be ingested to expedite the recovery process. Ideally, a recovery strategy that calls for 0.5 grams of carbohydrate per pound of body weight should continue every two hours for the six to eight hours following the session. For example: A 200-lb. athlete should consume approximately 100 grams of carbohydrates every two hours for at least six hours following heavy training or a game.

The commercial high-carbohydrate/electrolyte (minerals) sports drinks are fine, especially for that initial 15-minute post-exercise period. The palatability of these drinks sometimes encourages a higher usage over plain water, enabling the athletes to get more of what they need in their bodies.

A distinction should be made among carbohydrates that have a low, moderate, or high glycemic index. The glycemic index is a ranking of foods by their ability to introduce glucose to the blood. This glycemic response is predicated on factors such as the food's fiber and fat contents, the amount eaten, and its preparation. The higher the index number, the quicker the glucose enters the bloodstream. Illustration 2 presents the glycemic index rankings for some popular carbohydrate foods.

Illustration #2

GLYCEMIC INDEX OF POPULAR FOODS (Based on 50 grams of Carbohydrates per Serving)		
HIGH	**MODERATE**	**LOW**
Glucose 100	Muffin, bran..............60	Apple.....................36
Gatorade 91	Bran Chex...............58	Pear........................36
Potato, baked 85	Orange Juice............57	Power Bar............30-35
Corn Flakes 84	Potato, boiled............56	Chocolate Milk.........34
Rice Cakes 82	Rice, white, long grain..56	Fruit yogurt, low fat....33
Potato, microwaved 82	Rice, Brown............55	Chick-peas..............33
Jelly Beans 80	Popcorn.................55	Lima beans, frozen......32
Vanilla wafers...........77	Corn......................55	Split Peas, Yellow......32
Cheerios.................74	Sweet Potato............54	Skim Milk..............32
Cream of wheat.........74	Pound Cake Sara Lee...54	Apricots, dried..........31
Watermelon.............72	Banana, overripe.........52	Banana, underripe......30
Bagel, Lender's White..72	Peas, green..............48	Green Beans............30
Bread, White............70	Baked Beans............48	Lentils....................29
Bread, whole wheat.65-75	Rice, white, parboiled..47	Kidney beans............27
Soft drink, Fanta........68	Lentil Soup..............44	While milk..............27
Mars Bar.................68	Orange....................43	Barley.....................25
Grape-Nuts..............67	All-Bran Cereal.........42	Grapefruit...............25
Couscous................65	Spaghetti (no sauce)....41	Fructose.................23
Table Sugar.............65	Pumpernickel Bread....41	
Raisins....................64	Apple Juice, Unsweet..41	
Oatmeal..............42-75		
Ice cream............36-80		

Foods having a high (above 60) glycemic index are better for post-practice/competition meals and energy enhancers during competition. The low (less than 40) to moderate (40-60) glycemic index foods are more appropriate for pre-practice/competition meals. Remember these are suggestions, not mandates etched in stone. Any type of carbohydrate source is better than none at all.

Carbohydrate summary: The FGP recommends 6-11 servings of the bread, cereal, rice and pasta group. Another 3-5 servings of vegetables and 2-4 servings of fruits will enable the athlete to meet the recommended 60-70% carbohydrate daily intake. These are crucial, high-energy foods that should be priorities on the athlete's grocery list.

Protein

No nutrient is steeped in as much myth as protein. From perusing the muscle magazines, you would assume that the average diet was severely protein deficient, or that athletes couldn't possibly get enough of the right type of protein from mere food. Nothing could be farther from the truth.

Protein should consist of approximately 15% of the daily calorie intake. As you will see this is not a difficult task to achieve. In reality most people consume far more than that.

Protein is comprised of any number of what are called amino acids. There are a possible 21 amino acids that the body needs to build tissue, though not all proteins contain the entire series. Nine of these amino acids (histidine, lysine, tryptophan, phenylalanine, methionine, valine, isoleucine, threonine, and leucine) are termed essential, because we must obtain them from food.

The remaining twelve (alanine, asparagine, aspartic acid, cysteine, cystine, glutamic acid, glycine, proline, glutamine, arginine, serine, and tyrosine) are called non-essential – not because we don't need them, but because our bodies can make them, if necessary.

Dairy products, fish, poultry, meat, and other animal sources are called complete proteins, because they contain 8-9 of the essential amino acid complex. Diets high in these food sources are certain to provide more than adequate amounts of quality protein.

While the exact protein needs for every individual have not yet been determined by science, researchers have been able to define some safe and workable guidelines. We know that active people need more than the Recommended Daily Allowance (RDA) of 0.4 grams of protein per pound of body weight (Lemon, 1995; Tarnopolsky *et al.*, 1992). Very active individuals and/or competitive athletes may need anywhere from 0.6-0.9 grams of protein daily. It is believed that amounts higher than 0.9 grams of protein per pound of body weight daily are unusable.

Is there a legitimate concern with the high saturated fat in many meat and dairy products? You can't completely avoid the saturated fat in these sources, but wiser choices can control it. A good rule of thumb when purchasing or ordering beef is to ask for loin or round. For pork, leg and loin are better choices. When looking for dairy products, choose the low fat varieties and those made with skim milk or non-fat powdered milk.

Many athletes operate under the erroneous assumption that

protein overload is required for muscle gains. For muscle growth, adequate protein, carbohydrate, and an appropriate strength-training regimen are required. The carbohydrates provide the fuel for the energy needed to engage in muscle-building resistance training, while protein aids in the repair and growth of the affected tissues. However, if you displace the needed carbohydrate with excess protein, you will fail to provide the body with its main energy source. In addition you may deprive the body of the many health-protective components in carbohydrates *(i.e.,* vitamins and minerals), especially those found in fruit and vegetable sources.

Protein Summary: Athletes should focus on consuming the healthier, high-quality protein choices. Keep in mind that the maximum usable amount is 0.9 grams per pound of body weight per day – an easily obtainable goal. Regarding protein and/or amino acid supplementation, remember that strength training – not exorbitant amounts of protein – is the variable for muscle growth.

Fats

The mere word conjures up a host of negative images, but believe it or not, certain fats are essential nutrients. Approximately 25-30% of the daily diet should be comprised of fat. While it is true that eating excessive amounts of fat – primarily saturated fat – can be unhealthy, other types of fat serve vital functions. A short list includes: maintaining skin and hair, protecting organs, storing and transporting the fat soluble vitamins (A, D, E, and K), securing cell walls, and insulating the body.

Fats are classified as saturated or unsaturated by the formation of fatty acids in their chemical structure. Saturated fats are among the most common in our diet, as they are found in meat, poultry, whole dairy foods, and tropical oils like palm and coconut. They are solid at room temperature. Without question a diet high in saturated fats is linked to many health detriments, including cardiovascular disease and some forms of cancer.

Many of the snack and fast foods young people munch on are loaded with saturated fat. Not only are these foods unhealthy, but they also provide little assistance in energy production for most sports. We ask our athletes to read the labels of their snack foods to find the saturated fat content. As a rule of thumb, if it reads more than 1-2 grams of saturated fat per serving, we suggest that they find something else to eat.

Unsaturated fats are derived from both plant and animal-sources and are subdivided into monounsaturated and polyunsaturated forms. Monounsaturated fats are found mostly in vegetable oils (olive, canola, and peanut). Polyunsaturated fats are found in various nuts, fish, and also vegetable oils (safflower, sunflower, and soybean). Linoleic acid and alpha-linolenic acid (essential fatty acids in many of the body's functions) are derived from unsaturated fat sources (especially the omega-3 and omega-6 families found in many types of fish).

A word to the wise: Substitute fish (especially salmon, mackerel, and herring) for red meat every now and then in order cut back on saturated fat intake and to obtain these essential fatty acids.

Fats Summary: While fats are not necessarily the portrayed grim reapers of nutrition, moderation is the operative word. The paramount objective is to stay within the 25-30% daily recommendation and to keep most of that in the unsaturated fat category.

Vitamins and Minerals

Vitamins and minerals are the micronutrients in our diets and they serve the body with many vital processes. Vitamins are organic compounds that have numerous functions in growth and metabolism. Think of them as catalysts that regulate biochemical reactions in your body. Since our bodies cannot produce vitamins, we must obtain them from food. Contrary to popular belief the typical diet offers more than enough of the daily vitamin requirements. A vitamin is classified as either fat-soluble (A, D, E, and K) or water-soluble (C and the B complex) depending on which it uses to carry out its intended functions.

Important point: Vitamins in themselves do not provide energy. Instead they enable the body to derive energy from food. This knowledge should discourage athletes from assuming that it is acceptable to miss a meal as long as they pop a vitamin pill. Athletes who consume adequate calories are probably fulfilling their vitamin needs. Vitamin deficiencies are rare in diets that focus on the recommended guidelines presented in the FGP.

Minerals are inorganic elements that are present in all living cells. Their purpose is to regulate the speed of various reactions in the body and to maintain both the water and acid-base balance in our systems. Calcium, potassium, phosphorous, magnesium, iron, sodium, chromium, selenium, and zinc combine in many ways to form structures (bones and teeth) and accommodate vital functions (transport oxygen in the blood, assist in muscle contractions and nerve transmissions, and promote tissue healing /growth).

Vitamin and mineral summary: Vitamins and minerals are necessary components in a healthful diet, and our nutritional needs can easily be met by adhering to the recommendations of the FGP. There is little, if any, danger in taking a daily, over-the-counter vitamin/mineral supplement as an insurance policy. However we would strongly recommend that you check with your family physician before engaging in any of the mega-dose strategies promoted by various sources.

Water: Nature's Supplement

Water is the most required nutrient in our diets. It is involved in nearly every bodily function. The often heard recommendation of eight 10-12 ounce glasses of water per day may be fine for the average, sedentary individual – but athletes probably need more.

When counseling our athletes, we ask them to monitor their urine. If properly hydrated they should urinate approximately every two to four hours and their urine should be pale in color. Dark, concentrated urine is usually a red flag for inadequate water in the system and could be an indicator of dehydration.

Fluid intake should be an ongoing process. During strenuous exercise, practice, or games, at least 8-10 ounces of water or a non-carbonated sports drink should be consumed every 15-20 minutes. We provide our players with the choice of a non-carbonated sports drink or bottled water and make it readily available at all times. Post-exercise fluid intake should be approximately one quart per 1,000 calories expended. That sounds like a lot but it is needed and should be done gradually over a period of several hours.

Reading Food Labels

The Food and Drug Administration (FDA) now requires very helpful and informative labeling on food packaging (illustration #3). We encourage our athletes to check these labels in order to help them make wise food decisions.

Nutrition Facts

Serving Size 1 packet cereal (28g)
Servings Per Container 12

Amount Per Serving

Calories	100
Calories from Fat	0

	% Daily Value*
Total Fat 0g	**0%**
Saturated Fat 0g	**0%**
Cholesterol 0mg	**0%**
Sodium 170mg	**7%**
Potassium 25mg	**1%**
Total Carbohydrate 21g	**7%**
Dietary Fiber 1g	**4%**
Sugars 0g	
Other Carbohydrate 20g	
Protein 3g	

Vitamin A 25%	•	Vitamin C 0%
Calcium 20%	•	Iron 45%
Thiamin 25%	•	Riboflavin 20%
Niacin 25%	•	Vitamin B₆ 25%
Folate 25%		

* Percent Daily Values are based on a 2,000 calorie diet. Your daily values may be higher or lower depending on your calorie needs:

		Calories:	2,000	2,500
Total Fat	Less than		65g	80g
Sat Fat	Less than		20g	25g
Cholesterol	Less than		300mg	300mg
Sodium	Less than		2,400mg	2,400mg
Potassium			3,500mg	3,500mg
Total Carbohydrate			300g	375g
Dietary Fiber			25g	30g

The first point of emphasis is the serving size, which is provided in familiar units: cups, pieces, and the metric amount (grams). These serving sizes are based upon the amount of food people typically eat, thus making them realistic and easily comparable to similar foods. All of the information at the top of the label is dependent on the serving size not necessarily the contents of the package. The entire package may actually contain several servings, which adds to the numbers indicated on the label.

Note to the calorie conscious athlete: One gram of fat equals 9 calories, one gram of carbohydrate equals 4 calories, and one gram of protein equals 4 calories. You can purchase a calorie counter at most grocery stores to help you keep track of calorie intake.

Some food label highlights: Check the % Daily Value (DV) column on the far right of the food label. While it is based on a 2,000 calorie per day diet (many athletes, especially large males, consume much more than that), the numbers can still assist you with making healthier food choices.

A rule of thumb when attempting to decipher this information is that 5% or less is considered low for that particular nutrient, and 20% or more is considered to be on the high end. This knowledge will assist you in determining how *good or bad* the food is from a health standpoint when examining the total fat, saturated fat, cholesterol, and sodium categories per serving.

Obviously it would be wise to stick to foods (especially snacks) that are in the 5%-15% range per serving in those areas. Conversely, you should search for foods that have a higher DV% in the carbohydrate, vitamin, and mineral listings. Neither sugars nor protein list a DV%. In the case of sugars no DV% has been established because no recommendations have been made for the total amount to be eaten each day. Keep in mind that the sugars listed on the label include the naturally occurring ones (as in fruit and milk) as well as those added to the food.

Protein intake is not believed to be a concern for adults and children over four years of age, thus there is no listed DV%. The exception is when a food claim such as *high protein* is made, which requires a DV% listing.

You will notice that vitamins A and C, and the minerals calcium and iron have earned their own special slots on the label. This of course is due to their importance in the diet and the fact that many individuals must track their daily intake of these nutrients.

Caution is the operative word when terms like *reduced fat, light,* and *low fat* is emblazoned on the label in neon-like colors.

Reduced fat simply means that the food has 25% less fat than the manufacturers regular brand of that same food. If the regular brand is very high in fat to begin with, the 25% reduction doesn't necessarily make the reduced fat version healthy as many people assume.

Light means that the food has 50% less fat than the original version. The total fat in the original version is the telling tale.

Low fat means that the product has 3 grams of fat per serving of two tablespoons. Be sure to check the saturated fat line as that is the type of fat you want to keep as low as possible.

Gaining Good Weight

The majority of inquires we receive on nutrition deal with gaining weight. It seems that everyone is searching for a special diet or mystical elixir for packing-on the muscle. A sound strength-training program, in conjunction with a sensible nutrition strategy that is predicated on the Food Guide Pyramid (FGP), is the variable in gaining muscle weight. This is not to say that a balanced caloric intake cannot be given a *boost* with one of the so-called *supplements* currently on the market. However, the truth remains that it is very much possible to get the needed amount of daily calories and nutrients from whole food.

If an athlete is having difficulty gaining or maintaining good weight, the following simple daily caloric intake formula should be put into effect: Current body weight x 19 or 20.

For example: A 200-lb. athlete who is attempting to gain or maintain his current body weight should be consuming between 3,800 and 4,000 calories per day. The approximate breakdown of those calories is 65% carbohydrate, 15% protein, and 20% fat. Slight adjustments can be made as time elapses (BW x 21 calories), depending on the desired results.

Supplements

Hardly a day goes by without one of our athletes asking a question on supplementation. We believe in following the basics and not becoming enamored with the plethora of supplements and their questionable claims. However, we do understand that athletes will at times benefit from a liquid calorie boost. This is especially true when the team is on the road or playing double-headers and convenience is a major issue. We provide our athletes with recovery and energy drinks that contain the appropriate balance of protein, carbohydrate, vitamins, and minerals. Reputable and proven companies that have many years of research behind their products have developed these drinks. Feel free to contact me for further information on these products.

If you choose to purchase supplements, be fully aware of what you're getting. The label on a dietary supplement must contain enough information regarding the composition of the product to enable the buyer to make an informed decision. The manufacturer is responsible for assuring that the product is safe and the listed information is truthful and not misleading in any way.

Creatine has been a hot topic in the supplement world for many years. The NCAA prohibits its athletic departments from distributing it. My personal view on creatine is that I would like to see more long-term research performed on it before I wholeheartedly endorse it. While it is a naturally occurring substance in many food sources (primarily meat and fish products), I am not comfortable at this time with recommending it as a supplement.

Unfortunately some supplements are in a *buyer-beware* market. Manufacturers and distributors do not need to register with the FDA or get FDA approval to produce and sell dietary supplements. Any supplements that contain ingredients that might pose potential health problems should clearly indicate these concerns on the label.

Finally it is imperative that collegiate athletes compare the listed ingredients on any supplement they are considering with the *NCAA List of Banned Substances* to make sure they are in compliance with the rules. High school associations in some states may have similar rules and regulations regarding banned substances in supplements, and the coaches must disseminate this information to their athletes.

Before taking a supplement, you should ask the following questions:

◆ Why do I need a supplement? Could it be that my current dietary habits are inadequate?

◆ Have you checked the research and/or consulted with your parents, coaches, athletic trainer, or physician on the safety and efficacy of the supplement you are considering?

◆ Do you want to take the supplement simply because a friend takes it, or you have been influenced by a big-name endorser of the product? Are these legitimate reasons to take a supplement?

◆ Does the label on the product list all of its ingredients? Have you checked the label for potentially dangerous and/or illegal/banned substances?

◆ Does this supplement have any potential, negative side effects (e.g., can it exacerbate a state of dehydration in hot weather)?

Additional word of caution: Be wary about ordering a supplement over the web, as you have no guarantee regarding the contents and safety of the product.

References

1. American Dietetic Association and Canadian Dietetic Association, Position of the American Dietetic Association and Canadian Dietetic Association, Nutrition for physical fitness and athletic performance, *Journal of the American Dietetic Association*, 93:691-696, 1993.

2. Lemon, P.M., Do Athletes Need More Protein And Amino Acids? *International Journal of Sports Nutrition,* (Supplement): S39-S61, 1995.

3. Tarnopolsky, J., *et al.*, Evaluation of Protein Requirements For Trained Strength Athletes, *Journal of Applied Physiology,* 73(5): 1986-1995, 1992.

Ken Mannie

Strength/Conditioning Coach
Michigan State University

Ken Mannie is currently in his eighth year as the Head Strength and Conditioning Coach at Michigan State University. He spent nine years in the same capacity at The University of Toledo, Ohio, prior to joining MSU, and worked the high school level for ten years as a Health/Physical Education teacher and coach for football, wrestling, track, and strength/conditioning.

In 1974 Ken received his Bachelor's Degree in Health/Physical Education from the University of Akron in Ohio. He received his Masters Degree from Ohio State University in Physical Education with an emphasis in Exercise Science in 1985. He became a Certified Strength/Conditioning Specialist (CSCS) with the National Strength and Conditioning Association in 1986, and a Certified Strength and Conditioning Coach (SCCC) with the Collegiate Strength and Conditioning Coaches Association (CSCCa) in 2001.

In 2002 he became a Master Strength and Conditioning Coach with the CSCC, which is the highest honor a collegiate strength and conditioning coach can receive. It represents professionalism, knowledge, experience, expertise, and longevity in the field.

Ken has written over 100 articles on strength/conditioning, skill development, nutrition, drug abuse, and motivation for numerous publications. He has authored three book chapters, and writes a monthly column for *Scholastic Coach and Athletic Director*, the nation's premier coaching publication. He is also a frequent contributor to the *Championship Performance Newsletter.*

Ken and his wife, Marianne, have a daughter, Alaina, 14.

You can reach Ken at: Ken Mannie, Strength/Conditioning Coach, Michigan State University, Duffy Daugherty Bldg, East Landsing, MI 48824 or e-mail him at: mannie@msu.edu.

CHAPTER 12

Performance Enhancing Supplements

Terry Keigher and Gary Birchell

No book on improving baseball performance would be complete without a chapter on steroids and performance-improving supplements. Most fans of baseball are concerned about the growing use of steroids. Some feel that the use of these drugs constitutes cheating. A greater concern, however, is the long-term health effect on the user of the products as athletes can become physically and psychologically dependent on these drugs.

Ideally as we have tried to show throughout this book, enhanced performance can be achieved through hard work and unique physical and mental training methods. Steroids take things to the next level. There is no question that they work, and the rationale for their use is that the athlete is simply putting something into his or her body that is already there anyway. What harm is it if they take a substance that naturally raises a level of something that is already in their body – testosterone? While most sports allow the use of vitamins, protein powders and high energy sport drinks, they draw the line on the use of steroids or steroid-like substances. The rationale is that steroids are unnatural because they raise levels in the body to above-normal ranges. To many this is unnatural and considered cheating.

The moral and ethical issue that comes up with the use of steroids is this: If it is unnatural for a sprinter to raise the testosterone level in his body from high-normal to two times normal to enhance performance, is it also unnatural for a sprinter with a low level of testosterone in his system to use supplements that bring his levels to the high side of normal? That is the issue this chapter will discuss.

For some the answer is simple. Any substance put into the human body to enhance performance by raising testosterone levels is wrong. To others bringing low levels of testosterone in the human body to the high-normal range through the use of certain pro-hormone products is not cheating and advisable. Pro-hormone products are products sold off the shelf that naturally raise testosterone levels in the human body. They are not banned substances by most sport groups and are believed to possibly level the playing field a bit.

Healthcare Foundation

The first part of this chapter will deal with the opinion of the Healthy Competition Foundation *(www.healthycompetition.org)*, founded by the Blue Cross And Blue Shield Association. The Foundation's position is that use of all steroid or steroid-related products is potentially harmful to the human body and not acceptable in sports competition. What the Healthy Competition Foundation hopes to do is educate young people and their families about the potential health dangers of performance-enhancing drugs and to eliminate their use at all levels of sports.

According to the Foundation most supplement products available over-the-counter or on the Internet contain androstenedione (andro), creatine or ephedra. These products are not regulated or tested by the FDA and some have been reported to cause negative health consequences ranging from cramps or headaches to acne and kidney problems. The Healthy Competition Foundation supports drug-free competition without the use of these products. The Foundation recommends that athletes of all ages consult with their doctor before taking a supplement containing andro, creatine, ephedra or related substances.

Although most negative health-related effects of steroid use are anecdotal, the Healthy Competition Foundation believes there is strong evidence that steroid use is harmful to the athlete's body. It is apparent that young athletes today are not thinking in terms of health risks but only of improved performance and increased muscle bulk. According to the Healthy Competition Foundation there are several health-related consequences of using steroids that athletes should be aware of. Here are a few of them.

- ◆ **Changes in Appearance** – Acne and oily skin are extremely common results from steroid use. Another would be change in hair growth. Hair begins to grow everywhere but on the head, and the chances of increased male pattern baldness is prevalent. Men may also develop larger breasts, and women could see breast shrinkage.

- ◆ **Muscle Injury** – There have been various annual studies that have shown that tendons may rupture more easily with steroid use. Ligaments are also subject to the same problems as tendons. Steroid use could be contributing to the increasing percentage of professional baseball players who end up on the disabled list.

- ◆ **Changes in Fertility** – Most athletes on high doses of steroids have fertility problems. A large percentage of steroid users will notice a reduction in the size of their testicles.

- ◆ **Increased Risk of Heart Disease or Stroke** – Long term use of steroids has been shown to affect HDL and LDL cholesterol levels by reducing the good HDL levels and increasing the bad LDL cholesterol levels.

- ◆ **Increased Risk of Developing Prostrate Cancer** – Steroids add testosterone to the body so this is extremely negative for someone who may be predisposed to prostate cancer. A common method of treating prostrate cancer is to reduce testosterone levels in the body. Sometimes the female hormone estrogen is added to help accomplish this.

◆ **Increased Risk of Liver Disease** – Since steroids are filtered through the liver, it is understandable that they could negatively affect the liver. Jaundice, hepatitis and liver tumors all increase with the use of steroids.

◆ **Increased Aggression** – Increased levels of testosterone from steroid use have shown to increase aggression in athletes.

◆ **Dependency** – While much of the negative results of steroid use can be reversed by stopping their use, it is also common that many athletes develop a psychological dependency to steroids and find it very difficult to stop using them.

Certainly the negative health affects of steroid use are evident. *The Healthy Competition Foundation* is against all steroid use and even recommends against the use of creatine.

Product Manufacturer

A manufacturer of performance-enhancing sport supplements offers another point of view. Their position is that it is possible to get *sane* steroid-like results from the use of sport supplements. They use the term *sane* steroid-like results because it is impossible to get results from over-the-counter supplements that are comparable to the massive doses of steroids that some athletes are using today.

High school ballplayers and major leaguers sometimes use these pre-cursors or pro-hormone products, but the NCAA bans them. T.C. Luoma of Biotest Laboratories and *Testosterone Magazine* identified several of their products that baseball players could benefit from. Luoma believes that their protein power, *Grow,* would be beneficial to any ballplayer. Scientists estimate that intense exercise increases protein requirements by as much as 200% over the recommended daily allowance (RDA). *Grow* is designed to be a high protein meal replacement product for athletes who want to maximize muscle mass, lose fat, or increase athletic performance, but keep carbohydrates to a minimum.

Biotest's *Power Drive* product is designed to enhance neurotransmitter function, thus increasing concentration and performance. *Power Drive* contains the ingredients L-Tyrosine and Phosphatidylcholine. Studies performed by Dr. Jeffrey Stout of Creighton University found that tyrosine, when administered about an hour before working out, increased peak torque by an average of 28.3% during a set of 15 leg extensions. In short the evidence is strong that supplemental tyrosine can improve performance as well as increase energy levels, mental ability and the sense of well-being. Phosphatidylcholine has been shown to increase levels of another vital neurotransmitter known as acetylcholine. This potent neurotransmitter has been implicated in controlling motor unit recruitment, reflex and reaction times, as well as memory.

Their *Biotest Surge* product, which they recommend players drink after actual performance, is a superior sport drink that helps speed up the body's recovery time. This product would be especially beneficial to pitchers. All these products would be approved for use by high school and college athletes. Biotest's testosterone enhancing product, *Tribex 500*, is designed to stimulate the body to increase testosterone levels to the higher range of normal. *Mag10* and *4AD-EC*, work as well as a *sane* dose of steroids.

Biotest appears to be a science-driven company not afraid to push the envelope in the sports supplement field. When asked if use of his products constituted cheating, Luoma said, "Products that bring endocrine levels to beyond-normal levels could probably be considered cheating, whereas products that just get endocrine levels to optimum normal range would not be considered cheating. Our products are very popular in football, hockey and track, but less so in baseball, although we have several well-known players using our products. For some reason baseball has been several years behind the curve when it comes to supplements and training, and some innovative coaches and mangers are just beginning to catch up. Hopefully this book will give them some positive ideas they can get behind."

The Middle Ground

Gary Birchell, a certified trainer and nutritionist in Florida, supplies a third point of view on this subject. Here are his thoughts:

I have a slightly different philosophy when it comes to supplementation. First of all, I believe every ballplayer should understand basic nutrition. This is Level One. Ken Mannie's chapter in this book is a great place to start. A ballplayer needs to understand the basics of proteins, essential fats and carbohydrates. He also needs to understand the basics of proper water intake and why it is so important. After he learns the basics of proper eating and drinking, I usually recommend a good multi-vitamin. You need to keep in mind that ballplayers usually have greater nutrient needs than the average person, especially with something like vitamin C. In the resource section at the back of this book you can find some good suggestions, but I usually recommend GNC's Ultra-Mega Gold to athletes because it is designed for athletic individuals. I also like the fact that it is time-released giving the body what it needs in smaller, more usable doses versus dose-dumping large amounts of vitamins and minerals into the body all at one, which ends up being excreted through urine. Lifesource's three times a day Multi-Vite is also excellent. You can get more information on their product in the back of this book. Once these are part of an athlete's lifestyle, I would proceed to Level Two.

Level Two begins with protein powders and meal replacement powders and drinks. These high protein powder meals in a package give a ballplayer the enhanced nutrients his body needs and often doesn't get from his regular three meals a day. A lot of ballplayers don't get enough protein in their normal diets, and these meal replacement products offer a good source of protein with a higher biological value critical to athletes for muscle tissue repair and recovery.

Biotest's *Power Drive* is a great pre-game supplement for improved focus and concentration. For after games or training, a good anti-oxidant is highly recommended to reduce free radical damage within the body. Any anti-oxidant you use should include Vitamins A, C, and E, Selenium, Zinc, Alpha Lipoic Acid, Green Tea, Co Q-10 and even Grape Seed Extract.

At Level Two we may also put a ballplayer on creatine. In my opinion creatine has been very thoroughly researched and most studies I've seen have been supportive of its use. Five grams a day is usually enough to add several pounds of lean mass to a ballplayer.

Glutamine, the most abundant amino acid in muscle tissue, might also be added. Glutamine is rapidly depleted through intense physical activity, and it needs to be replaced in order for protein synthesis to occur at optimal levels. It is also important for a healthy immune system.

If we are trying to take off some weight, I've found that CLA or conjugated linoleic acid often does a good job of reducing abdominal fat. In a recent study published in the *International Journal of Obesity* (August 2001), it showed that participants taking CLA lost an average of 1.4 cm in waist circumference after only four weeks. Several additional studies have shown that CLA reduces body fat while maintaining lean muscle mass. CLA also has been shown to help protect against many diseases including atherosclerosis and cancer. Usually three grams a day over a three-month period will show some positive results.

At Level Three we enter into the gray area (or unproven or untested area) of supplementation. There is a lot of manufacturer hype and a lot of claims, but we really haven't seen a lot of testing. The area I'm speaking of is the pro-hormone area. Some of Biotest's products would fall into this category. There is good science backup to the first two levels of supplementation. In the third level, however, there really isn't a lot of science. Some ballplayers claim great results and others do not. While the NCAA has banned pro-hormone use, many of these products do not send up any red flags. They can also become quite expensive for a young ballplayer.

As for steroids, I've stayed away from them for a lot of the same reasons the Healthy Competition Foundation is against them. There is no question that steroids work. They also make it much easier to recover from a workout as it probably triples the recovery time. One main problem I see with steroids, however, is that muscle gains come so quickly that the body's tendons and ligaments can't handle it.

I'm glad that baseball is finally beginning to address the steroid issue. Right now professional ballplayers are sending out a very bad message to young ballplayers. It might take a little longer to get to the top with good nutrition and legal supplementation, but I think a ballplayer can do it. He might not be quite as strong or as fast as someone might be on steroids, but he'll be a lot healthier for it down the road.

Terry Keigher and Gary Birchell

Contributors

The Blue Cross and Blue Shield Association founded the Healthy Competition program to educate young athletes, parents and coaches about the potential health risks of performance-enhancing drugs and sports supplements. The Healthy Competition program's philosophy is that skill, dedication, and hard work are the most important qualities for success in sports and life. Terry Keigher is Manager, Corporate Sponsorships for Blue Cross and Blue Shield Association.

You can reach Terry Keigher and the Healthy Competition Foundation at: www.healthycompetition.org, phone, 312-297-5824, e-mail: terry.keigher@bcbsa.com.

Gary Birchell is a Certified Personal Trainer with over ten years of experience in the Central Florida area. He specializes in preparing grade school and college athletes of all sports for the next level of competition. He excels in working around sports related injuries and creating muscle balance that in-turn prevents future problems. Gary also prepares sport and athlete specific nutrition and supplementation programs that gives athletes a distinct advantage on the playing field. A former athlete, drug-free bodybuilder and mens fitness competitor, Gary resides in Lake Mary, Florida with his wife and four children.

Gary Birchell, Naturally Fit, voicemail, 407-400-3025, e-mail: glbdarling@aol.com.

CHAPTER 13

Weight Training For Baseball

Kerry Rosenboom
Wichita State University

In the game of baseball, some things will never change. For as long as I can remember, the pitching mound has always been 60 feet 6 inches away from home plate, and three strikes means you're out. At the same time the game has undergone some drastic changes. Baseball has become a game of technology and specialization, where camcorders and computers are as important as scouting reports.

While some changes are welcomed, others are met with great resistance. The best example of this is weight training, especially as it relates to baseball players. Over the last ten years it has been one of baseball's most controversial topics. It is an area full of myths and misconceptions, such as:

- *Baseball players should not lift weights during the season, it will tire them out.*

Actually the exact opposite is true! The reason that baseball players lift during the season is to maintain their strength throughout the long grueling season. An in-season weight program is a valuable asset, regardless of your position. As a pitcher you will see improved velocity, as well as improved endurance. Endurance is important in two areas. First, you need to sustain your average first-inning velocity into at least the sixth or seventh inning. Second, you must be as strong at the end of the season as you were at the beginning of the year. A good in-season weight-training program will do these things, as well as help to improve recovery time and decrease the chance of injury. A position player will be able to maintain his bat speed and arm strength. With a good in-season weight program, you should feel as quick and strong at the end of the season as you do at the start.

◆ *You should only lift light weights. Heavy weights*
   will bind you up.

This myth can become a reality if you neglect a few key areas.
   1) *Flexibility Training* – You must stretch before and after every lifting season. This will not only help with your performance enhancement, but also with injury prevention.
   2) *Exercise Technique* – Improper-lifting technique is normally a result of lifting too much weight on a particular exercise. If you use the correct technique and remain consistent with your weight-training program, you will achieve the desired results.
   3) *Program Design* – You must follow a program that is designed specifically for baseball players. This is an area that we will discuss in greater detail later on in the chapter.

◆ *You should never lift on game day.*

This is an area that must be looked at from two different perspectives: that of a pitcher, and that of a position player.

   1) As a starting pitcher, you do not need to lift on game day. I have worked with many pitchers that have chosen to do some light lifting on the day that they pitch, but this is entirely up to each individual. A normal lifting schedule would be as follows:

Day 1 –   Pitch
Day 2 –   Light upper body workout
                Heavy lower body workout
Day 3 –   Off
Day 4 –   Medium upper body workout
                Medium lower body workout
Day 5 –   Off
Day 6 –   Pitch

Or

Day 1 –   Pitch
Day 2 –   Light upper body workout
Day 3 –   Heavy lower body workout
Day 4 –   Medium upper body workout
Day 5 –   Medium lower body workout
Day 6 –   Pitch

As a relief pitcher you must take a different approach to your in-season weight program. A starting pitcher can arrange his weight-training routine around his pitching schedule. A relief pitcher must have designated lifting days and be prepared to pitch whenever called upon. As a relief pitcher I suggest that you lift at least 6-8 hours before you might pitch, or after the game. Here are a couple of lifting schedules for relief pitchers.

Monday   –   Light upper body workout
Tuesday   –   Heavy lower body workout
Wednesday   –   Medium upper body workout
Thursday   –   Medium lower body workout
Friday   –   Light upper body workout
Saturday   –   Heavy lower body workout
Sunday   –   Off

Or

Monday   –   Light upper body workout
                         Heavy lower body workout
Tuesday   –   Off
Wednesday   –   Medium upper body workout
                         Medium lower body workout

Thursday	–	Off
Friday	–	Light upper body workout
		Heavy lower body workout
Saturday	–	Off
Sunday	–	Off

2) As a position player you can lift on game day with no ill effects. In my 16 years as a strength and conditioning coach, I would estimate that over 90% of all position players that I have worked with have lifted on game day. It is all a matter of getting your body used to a certain routine, and staying with it. If a position player lifts on the day of a game, I recommend that they do it at least five hours before the game, or after the game. A couple of options that a position player could follow in-season would be:

Monday	–	Upper body workout
Tuesday	–	Lower body workout
Wednesday	–	Upper body workout
Thursday	–	Lower body workout
Friday	–	Upper body workout
Saturday	–	Lower body workout
Sunday	–	Off

Or

Monday	–	Total body workout
Tuesday	–	Off
Wednesday	–	Total body workout
Thursday	–	Off
Friday	–	Total body workout
Saturday	–	Off
Sunday	–	Off

Most players do not understand the benefits of a sport-specific weight-training program. But at the same time most players do not understand the risk involved in doing a program that is not designed specifically for baseball players. You must always remember that you are not a power lifter or bodybuilder, you are a baseball player and you must train accordingly. With this in mind I have outlined my 12 favorite exercises for baseball players.

Cable Baseball

This exercise will help increase a player's arm strength, recovery time, and decrease his chance of injury. This is another great in-season exercise to increase the blood flow to the shoulder.

To perform Cable Baseball you should always remember:
- ◆ You want to simulate your throwing motion.
- ◆ Make sure that your arm goes through the full range of motion, don't short arm.
- ◆ Keep your elbow above your shoulder.
- ◆ Keep the front shoulder closed until your throwing arm comes forward.

Incline Dumbbell Bench

The incline dumbbell bench, in my opinion, is the best chest exercise that a baseball player can do. If your chest is strong and flexible, it will save your shoulder from a lot of wear and tear.

To perform this exercise you should:

- Sit back on the incline bench, keeping your back flat at all times.
- Start with the dumbbells raised directly over your shoulders.
- As you inhale, you will lower the dumbbells to the outside portion of your shoulders.
- Then exhale as you push the dumbbells back to the starting position.
- Make sure that at the top of the exercise you do not hit the dumbbells together. Over time this can cause trauma to the shoulders.

Incline Dumbbell Rows

Incline Dumbbell Rows will strengthen your lats, as well as your rear delts. This is vitally important as we work to maintain good muscle balance.

To perform this exercise you should:

- Lie face down on an incline bench.
- Hold a dumbbell in each hand with your thumbs facing forward.
- Pull the dumbbells straight up to your shoulders, keeping your elbows close to your sides as you go up.
- Return to the starting position making sure that your arms are totally straight at the bottom of the motion.

Seated Dumbbell Curls

This is an excellent biceps exercise. When performing any biceps exercise, make sure that you get full range of motion. If you don't get full extension at the bottom of each repetition, it can lead to problems in the lower biceps or elbow region.

To perform seated Dumbbell Curls correctly you should:
- ♦ Sit down on the end of a bench with your legs straight ahead of you at a 90-degree angle.
- ♦ Hold a dumbbell in each hand with your palms facing down.
- ♦ Curl the weight to your shoulders keeping your elbows at your sides.
- ♦ Lower the dumbbells back to the starting position in a very controlled manner.
- ♦ Stop for 1-2 seconds before starting the next repetition.

Reverse Pressdowns

This is one of the best exercises that a baseball player can do. It will strengthen the triceps, as well as increase blood flow to the elbow region.

To perform Reverse Pressdowns, you should:
- Stand in front of a pressdown unit or lat pulldown machine.
- Grab the bar using a reverse grip.
- Your hands should be approximately shoulder width apart.
- With your elbows locked at your sides extend your arms straight down.
- Reverse the pattern and return to the starting position.
- The movement should be very controlled at all times.

Bent-Over Raises (Bench)

This is one of the most important exercises for baseball players, especially pitchers. It isolates the rear delts – an area that is commonly neglected. This imbalance can lead to numerous shoulder problems.

To perform Bent-Over Raises you should:
- Lie face down on a flat bench.
- Hold a light dumbbell in each hand.
- With a slight bend at the elbow raise the dumbbell off the ground up to shoulder height.
- Slowly return the weights back to the starting position.

Standing Wrist Curls

There are many outstanding forearm exercises but my favorite one is standing wrist curls. They do a great job of strengthening the forearms as well as keeping blood flow to the area around the elbow. If a player is having elbow tenderness, I will combine standing wrist curls with reverse press-downs to help eliminate this problem.

To perform standing wrist curls, you should:
- ◆ Stand straight up, holding a bar behind you.
- ◆ Keep your arms straight and have your palms facing behind you.
- ◆ Let the bar roll down into your fingertips and then roll it back up.
- ◆ All the movement should be below the waist.

Leg Press

When your goal is to improve lower body strength and endurance, there is not a better exercise than the leg press. This is a very safe and effective exercise, regardless of your lifting experience.

To perform this exercise:
- ◆ Place your feet approximately shoulder width apart.
- ◆ Let the weight come down until your legs are at 90-degree angle, or a couple of inches lower.
- ◆ As you push your weight back to the starting position, make sure that you do not lock your legs at the top of the movement.

◆ Make sure that you inhale as the weight is coming down and exhale as you are pushing the weight back up.

1-Legged Leg Press

The 1-legged leg press is a perfect example of an exercise that has a carry-over effect onto the playing field. It can directly aid a pitcher with drive leg endurance, or a position player with running speed.

When you perform the 1-legged leg press you should:
◆ Follow the same guidelines that are used for the leg press.
◆ The only difference might relate to your foot placement. You can move your foot toward the center 2-4 inches, depending on where it is most comfortable for you.

Leg Curls

There is no doubt in my mind that this is the best exercise for the hamstrings. For all the work that we will do for our quads, leg curls are crucial in maintaining muscle balance. For best results you should do both double-leg and single-leg hamstring work.

To perform leg curls you should:
- ◆ Lie on your stomach, with the footpad approximately at the Achilles.
- ◆ In a very controlled manner curl the weight up to about a 90-degree angle and then back down.
- ◆ It should take 2 seconds to raise the weight and 2 seconds to lower the weight.
- ◆ If you have knee problems, bring the weight to approximately a 70-degree to 75-degree angle.

Medicine Ball: (1-Knee/Opposite)

Baseball is a game of rotation. Regardless if you're a hitter or a pitcher, drills that can improve your upper body and lower body rotation are critical for performance enhancement. One of my favorite drills is Medicine Ball (1-Knee/Opposite).

To perform this exercise you should:
- ◆ Kneel down on your left leg, with your right leg straight ahead of you bent at a 90-degree angle.
- ◆ Your partner will stand approximately 6 feet behind you.
- ◆ Your partner will throw the ball to the side on which your knee is down.
- ◆ With your arms straight out you will catch the ball, and in one motion rotate around and throw the ball back to your partner.
- ◆ Make sure that your arms stay straight throughout the whole exercise.
- ◆ When you are done switch legs and repeat this exercise on the other side.

Medicine Ball: (Hitting Station)

This is my favorite drill for hitters. It will strengthen and quicken the hips for increased power potential. This is the most sport-specific drill that we will do in the weight room.

To perform this exercise you should:

- ◆ Stand approximately 5 feet away from a hard surface, such as a cement wall, or some other type of surface that you can throw a medicine ball against.
- ◆ Start this exercise by holding a medicine ball at your back hip.
- ◆ As you simulate your swing, guide the medicine ball along your belt-line and drive it into the hard surface.
- ◆ This exercise should be done in a quick fashion stressing back hip rotation.

Each of these twelve exercises will train a specific area. This is crucial for muscle balance, as well as performance enhancement. But at the same time, you must realize that there are other exercises that are equally as important. For instance, if a pitcher is experiencing elbow tenderness, we might replace the current triceps exercise with 1-Arm Reverse Pulldowns. I know that this exercise is very beneficial for increasing blood flow to the area around the elbow. Other exercises that will be beneficial over the course of the year include:

1) Chest: Bench Press, Dumbbell Bench Press, Decline Bench

2) Back: Front Pulldowns, Cable Rows, 1-Arm Front Pulldowns, 1-Arm Dumbbell Rows, and Hyperextensions

3) Biceps: E-Z Bar Curls, Incline Dumbbell curls, Straight Bar Curls, and Cable Curls

4) Triceps: Pressdowns, Bar Kickbacks Cable Press, 1-Arm Reverse Pressdowns, and Bench Dips

5) Forearms: Wrist Curls, Reverse Wrist Curls, Rope Rolls, Dumbbell Wrist Curls, and Hammer Curls

6) Shoulders: Shoulder Program, Cable Upright Rows, Bar Shrubs, and Dumbbell Upright Rows

7) Quads: Half Squats, Full Squats, Dumbbell Step-Ups, Bench Squats, and 1-Legged Dumbbell Squats

8) Calves: Standing Toe Raises, Seated Toe Raises and Toe Raises (Leg Press)

9) Abdominals: Decline Abs, Crunches, Kick-Ins, 1-Leggged Kick-Ins, Contraction Abs and Leg Raises

10) Rotation Exercises: Russian Twist, Side-to-Sides, S.F.H., and other Medicine Ball Drills

11) Optional: Lunges, Side Lunges, Wall Squats, and the Rice Workout

Over the course of the season virtually every exercise will be beneficial in one way or another. Each exercise and rep scheme has a direct purpose as it relates to performance enhancement. Just remember that every pitcher is not going to throw 90 MPH, and every hitter is not going to hit 25 home runs. But if you work hard, and do the right things, you will make gains that translate into improved performance.

Kerry Rosenboom

Head Strength and Conditioning Coordinator
Wichita State University

Kerry Rosenboom, a Wichita, Kansas native, is in his fifteenth year as Head Strength and Conditioning Coordinator at Wichita State University. Rosenboom joined the WSU staff in September, 1987 as the interim strength and conditioning coordinator and was elevated to his present position of Head Strength and Conditioning Coordinator in December, 1987.

Kerry also runs his own consulting business of putting professional baseball players on year-round workouts. He chose to start this after turning down several major league opportunities as head strength and conditioning coach. He has trained over 40 players that have reached the major leagues, as well as over 30 pitchers that have thrown at least 95 MPH. Through his consulting business, he has worked with players that have received all-star recognition from rookie ball to the major leagues.

The 1982 graduate of Bishop Carroll High School in Wichita was named the 1997 and 1998 Missouri Valley Conference Strength and Conditioning Coach of the Year. He is in demand for lectures, seminars, and strength-training articles. He has been a guest speaker at the 1996 American Baseball Coaches Association annual meeting, the 1997 Baseball Bash and the Reebok Baseball Clinic. He also lectured at the Strength Coaches National Convention during the summer of 1993, and has had articles on weight training for pitchers and position players published in *Collegiate Baseball and Strength Coaches Journal.* Rosenboom was also a guest lecturer at the Syd Thrift Baseball Institute in the summer of 1989.

He earned his Bachelor of Science degree in Administration and Fitness and Management at Kansas Newman College, while lettering four years in baseball. He was named to the All-District 10 Honorable Mention Team as a relief pitcher in 1987, recording three saves in fifteen appearances. He finished his career at Kansas Newman that ranked in the top 10 in numerous career and single-season record categories. He is also a member of The National Strength and Conditioning Association, and is a Certified Level I Weight Lifting instructor.

Rosenboom, is married to the former Jean Leeker. The couple has three children, Kayla, Tyler and Katie.

You can reach Kerry at: kerryr@cox.net *or go to his web address at* www.weighttrainingforbaseball.com.

CHAPTER 14

How Vision Plays Into
Your Game

Barry L. Seiller, M.D.
Visual Fitness Institute

Sports vision is the facet of sports medicine that is dedicated to improving the visual skills that are needed to excel in athletic competition and sports activities. An athlete's vision plays an important part in how well he or she performs competitively and, just as exercise and practice, can increase the athlete's strength and speed; exercise and practice can improve an athlete's visual fitness. Under game conditions, vision training ranks right up there with weight training and conditioning.

Professional and amateur athletes often are remarkably skillful at adapting to their visual challenges and level of visual skills. Many athletes have good visual skills that enable them to play well but, if sharpened, could help them play even better. There can be no doubt that an athlete's visual skills (good or bad) will have a significant impact (positive or negative) on his or her overall performance. The medical and technical literature supports the assertion that athletes have better visual skills than non-athletes do.

Each sport requires different visual skills. These skills (many of which exist simultaneously) are interrelated but can be separated into individual components, measured, and either trained or enhanced. These individual components can then be reintegrated into a new visual orientation. Like any sport, baseball carries with it a unique set of requirements for the body and the eyes.

Baseball requires visually demanding skills that are position-specific. For example, pitchers must be able to locate pitches, pick off base runners, recognize signals from the catcher, and field bunts. On the other hand, batters require visual skills that allow them to accurately pick up the location and rotation of pitches, judge the speed of pitches, bunt effectively, and maintain balance. Fielders likewise, must have well-trained eyes in order to pick up the ball off the bat, get the jump on the ball, read ground balls and turn double plays.

A common misconception, among athletes and non-athletes alike, is that there is no discernable distinction between vision and *visual skills*. Vision is something we are born with, that can worsen over time, but that often can be corrected with the aid of glasses, contacts or surgery. Visual *skills*, like physical skills, can be taught, trained and practiced. How many times have you heard someone refer to a gifted athlete – perhaps a baseball catcher or a wide receiver – as having great hands? An athlete might have big hands, flexible hands or strong hands, but there is no such thing as great hands. It is a catchall term for a catcher or receiver whose performance is top-notch and consistent – an athlete with great hand-eye-body coordination. And this type of coordination is a skill that can be taught, over time and with practice, to any athlete, regardless of how big or flexible or strong his or her hands might physically be.

Visual Skills And Abilities

There are a variety of things that can be characterized as visual skills and abilities. A skill is something that can be refined by training, while an ability is something you are born with, but that can be enhanced. The following are key skills and abilities that a baseball player can and should measure, and seek to train or enhance:

- ◆ Eye alignment
- ◆ Depth perception
- ◆ Ocular flexibility
- ◆ Visual tracking
- ◆ Visual recognition time
- ◆ Speed of focusing
- ◆ Hand-eye-body coordination

Visual skills and abilities are unique to each individual. They are interrelated, but with today's technology can be isolated and measured. The combination of strengths and weaknesses in these categories determines what type of athlete someone is or will become. In order to deal with their inaccuracies, athletes develop compensatory mechanisms. These compensations get stronger over time; therefore, the younger the athlete, the easier it is to break down these habits and replace them with strengthened skills.

Keep Your Eye On The Ball

"Watch the ball...look at the ball." Coaches, trainers and parents say it all the time, but sometimes, it is easier said than done. It takes four tenths of a second for a 90-MPH fastball to travel the 60 feet, 6 inches from the pitcher to the plate. An athlete has two tenths of a second to decide whether to swing at the ball. That leaves just two tenths of a second to process the visual information. The athlete must recognize the type of pitched ball in order to identify such things as inside, outside, curveball, fastball, rotation and pace. These determinations are made as a result of visual information. Many high-level athletes can process that visual information even more quickly than at a rate of two tenths of a second, which gives them more time to adjust their swing. They process the information more efficiently because they have the born or learned ability to filter out the *clutter* that retards the processing speeds of other athletes. The most common cause of this distraction is inaccurate visual information. If that visual information is inaccurate, it often will cause the batter to swing early or late, foul the ball off, check the swing, or miss completely.

> # Keep Your Eye On the Ball!
>
> ## *Sometimes That's Easier Said Than Done!*
>
> *The ability of the batter to see the ball as it is released, track it to the plate, and hit it accurately, depends on excellent dynamic visual acuity and visual pursuit movements.*
>
> *The ability of the fielder to pick up the ball off the bat, determine the correct angle, track it accurately, and make the catch, requires excellent vision, depth perception, and eye/hand/body coordination.*
>
> **Visual Fitness Institute**

Eyesight

Eyesight, or visual acuity, can be divided into two categories. Static visual acuity, the ability to see a stationary target, is assessed by identifying numbers, letters or pictures of varying sizes. This is usually assessed in a doctor's office. This is the type of vision used for objects that have little motion. Static vision can be improved temporarily by a number of traditional methods, such as eyeglasses and contact lenses, or permanently with laser vision correction. Kinetic visual acuity, on the other hand, is the type of vision used when objects are in motion; it is the ability to resolve detail when there is relative movement between the observer and the test object. The skill of watching the ball as it is released from the pitcher's hand demands excellent static visual acuity (vision). Watching the ball to the plate, however, requires accurate tracking eye movements, shifting from far to near, in an attempt to never lose sight of the ball.

Eyeglasses: Eyeglasses have been used for centuries as the primary method of correcting poor vision. Glasses are easily accessible in many shapes, styles and sizes. Certain eyeglass frames are made for everyday use and are intended for social circumstances.

These types of glasses, however, are inappropriate for athletic activity, where they may slip, fall off or even break on impact. Corrective eyewear is available in various models with unbreakable lenses designed for sports activities.

Contact Lenses: Contact lenses, on the other hand, are well suited to sports activity and are available in two types. The first type is made of a rigid oxygen-permeable plastic material. Some athletes may find that, under certain conditions, this is the lens of choice. The advantages of these lenses are that they are infrequently in need of replacement and resist contamination. The primary disadvantage is unexpected sudden loss. If it is necessary for an athlete to wear this type of lenses, a spare pair is a necessity.

Soft contact lenses are currently the most popular type of lens, are available in most prescriptions, and come in non-disposable and disposable types. The disposable types are characterized by monthly, weekly or even daily wear protocols. Given the dusty environment wherein the game of baseball is played, disposability is paramount. Despite its slightly higher cost, the daily disposable is preferred. It requires no cleaning or storage, therefore saving time and eliminating the need for costly cleaning solutions. The fact that multiple pairs are available at any time reduces the concern over a lost, dirty or torn lens.

Laser Vision Correction: Correcting eyesight by using a laser to reshape the front surface of the eyeball is known as Lasik or photorefractive keratectomy (PRK), depending on the technique used. It is now a commonly accepted form of vision correction, and is reliable, precise, permanent and painless. Laser vision correction can replace glasses or contact lenses and can correct nearsightedness, farsightedness, astigmatism or a combination of these problems. Players can return to the field within a few days after the procedure; however, it is best undertaken in the off season. The athlete must be at least 18 years old to undergo the procedure, which is usually not covered by medical insurance. The average price varies. For more information, visit *www.seewithlasik.com*.

Kinetic Or Dynamic Acuity

Kinetic visual acuity is, as previously defined, eyesight while in motion, and is crucial when it comes to sports. Examples of the use of kinetic vision include a batter's attempting to hit a ball (the batter is stationary and the ball is in motion), a downhill skier's navigating a course (the course is stationary and the skier is in motion), and a tennis player's lobbing one over the net (both player and ball are in motion). More rapid and accurate eye movements can accomplish improvement in this skill. These movements can be trained by exercises that increase inward (convergent) and outward (divergent) movement of the eyes.

Eye Alignment

Most athletes' eyes don't line up exactly on a target even though the individual might believe that he or she is looking directly at that target. When this happens, the brain receives inaccurate information. Alignment will influence an athlete's perception of where the baseball is in free space.

A small amount of deviation is normal in most athletes. In reality, most people fixate left, right, above or below a sighted target; however, if a batter perceives the ball to be farther away than it actually is, he will swing the bat late. If a fielder does not fixate properly, the ball may get by him. It will also influence the ability to perceive the correct position of the baseball as it is pitched. It can likewise influence the batter's decision regarding when to swing.

Eye alignment cannot be trained directly, though certain exercises can reduce a small to moderate deviation. Reducing a deviation will change the perception of where an image is in space and, ultimately, can improve crucial and quantifiable things such as batting averages or caught balls.

Depth Perception

Depth perception or stereopsis (also known as 3-D or three-dimensional vision) is the ability to see an object in space. Along with other visual skills, it allows you to judge the object's speed and distance. The perception of depth relies on your ability to use both of your eyes simultaneously. The higher the level of collaboration between the eyes, the more precise is one's ability to hit or move appropriately. This skill is especially important for hitters and outfielders who must judge the distance, direction and speed of the ball, and react in a split second, under all lighting and weather conditions (sunlight, darkness, wind, domes). Depth perception cannot be trained. It can, however, be improved by improving an athlete's eyesight and by improving his or her eye alignment.

Visual Flexibility

Eye flexibility requires you to move your eyes together simultaneously and efficiently. Training the speed and efficiency of the two eyes moving together will allow the player to get his eyes on the ball quickly and accurately. Recognizing pitches early and having the time to decide whether to swing is truly the ability that makes the difference between victory and defeat. Ocular flexibility is an essential basis of hand-eye-body coordination.

Three distinct skills make up eye flexibility:
- ◆ Convergence — the ability of the eyes to maintain an inward posture.
- ◆ Divergence — the ability of the eyes to maintain an outward posture.
- ◆ Alternating flexibility — the ability to alternate between inward and outward postures.

Visual Tracking

Visual tracking is the ability to follow the ball in order to catch or hit it. Improving your visual tracking skills will enable you to scan the playing field better, allowing you to see, think and react more quickly. Visual tracking is trained by presenting simple visual targets to one eye and then to the other. This is followed by training both eyes together. The athlete must process the target and then make an accurate motor response. The targets vary in size and complexity in order to challenge the athlete's level of skill.

Visual Recognition

Well-developed visual recognition skills allow athletes to remember and react to what they see. Improving recognition and processing of visual information will help gain an edge over the competition. Visual recognition is the ability to see a target, remember it and reproduce it in a similar manner. It helps in remembering pitches that have been thrown previously and in knowing where fielders are positioned.

In order to train an athlete's visual recognition skills, visual targets are presented, beginning with a simple pattern and a reasonable amount of time to recognize the pattern. The athlete will practice the speed and accuracy at which he can accurately recognize and make appropriate motor responses to the displayed pattern. As the athlete improves this skill, the complexity and duration of the displayed patterns can be altered to increase the challenge.

Speed Of Focusing

Like other visual skills, the speed at which an athlete focuses can be trained and improved. Speed of focusing is trained by utilizing special prescription lenses that force the athlete to focus on given targets. Multiple repetitions of time and various types of targets are required to train this skill.

Hand-eye-body coordination is a combination of all of the primary visual skills working in harmony, which translates into more precise, accurate and quick movements. Turning a Little League player into a major league star requires the combination of many things – not just the synthesis of visual skills and abilities. There are perhaps five components to creating a superior baseball player:

1) Physical abilities (strength and size)
2) Psychological makeup and motivation
3) Mechanics
4) Conditioning
5) Visual skills and abilities, and visual confidence

If you compare two position players with comparable skills in the first four categories, the factor that will differentiate the two and make one more successful is visual skills. And barring any problem with the other four factors, it is those same visual skills that will ultimately fail them as they top out in the sport.

Dominant Eye

Everyone has a dominant and a non-dominant eye. The dominant eye is typically your strongest eye. To find your dominant eye, you can stretch your hands out and, crossing your two thumbs and two hands, leave a small opening similar to a frame. Keeping both eyes open, sight a small object in the frame. Close first one eye and see if the object is still present; open that eye and close the other eye and see if the object is still there. The eye with which you see the object in the frame is your dominant eye. This has nothing to do with being left-handed or right-handed. For many years players and coaches have thought that if you were batting right-handed and your leading eye (the left) was your dominant eye, you had an advantage. This was also thought to apply similarly to a left-handed batter who was right-eye dominant. Recently, this theory has been debunked and shown to be inaccurate. There appears to be no perceptible difference in batting averages in leading with your dominant or non-dominant eye. The most important factor is that your head is in a position to get both eyes on the ball.

Diagnosing visual skill deficiencies and developing a training regimen to improve those skills involves a combination of both low-tech and high-tech approaches. Even though all visual skills are inter-related, they can be separated in order to measure them. Once measured they can be compared to norms and graded. Once graded, a training program can be developed.

Vision training involves repetitive stimulation of brain centers in order to integrate a new visual orientation. It is unlike muscular exercise as it does not involve muscle memory and therefore the effect will be significantly longer lasting.

To improve eye alignment, depth perception and eye flexibility, athletes can do exercises with a piece of string laced with different colored beads. With the string stretched out in front of the face, an athlete shifts his or her focus between various beads, teaching the eye muscles to precisely hone in on targets with increasingly greater speed and accuracy. Exercises to improve hand-eye coordination involve hitting pegs on a board as they light up and measuring the speed at which the athlete can accurately perform. There are a variety of other low-tech approaches to vision fitness that can be performed at home for little to no cost. See the *Six Exercises You Can Do at Home to Improve Your Visual Skills* at the end of this chapter.

For the serious athlete, vision calisthenics have gone high-tech. With a computer, keyboard and joystick, it is now possible to train, measure and challenge vision skills in a customized regimen, whereby athletes replicate patterns that flash briefly on the screen or spot camouflaged shapes. Because vision performance training is something that benefits athletes not just during their off-season training bouts, but throughout their seasons, it is crucial that training tools, such as vision performance software like *the Visual Edge Performance Trainer™*, be available to athletes when they're on the road, in the locker room or at home. Not everyone has a Burnell Rotator for training visual motor skills, a Wayne Peripheral Awareness Trainer (the light board) or a Tachistoscope that flashes numbers and letters to train visual recognition time, but most everyone *does* have a desktop or laptop computer.

Weight training for the eyes is not all that different from sit-ups, bench presses or squats. Your workouts should be focused, consistent and long-term, and they'll leave you feeling much the same as any other exercise – slightly tired, mildly sore and a bit exhilarated about what you've just done to strengthen your body and improve your game.

Below are some frequently asked questions when it comes to vision training. The answers should help educate you as you prepare to incorporate vision performance training into your overall baseball-training regimen.

◆   *How often should I train?*
It is recommended that athletes train two to three times per week for 15 to 30 minutes.

◆   *Is it possible to over train?*
Just as with weight training, you can over train and develop fatigue.

◆   *Do the effects of vision training last?*
Certain training, such as hitting in a batting cage or against

rapidly thrown tennis balls, can help your timing, but like arm curls, if they are not done on a very regular basis, you lose the timing. We call this short-term visual memory. *If you don't use it, you lose it.* Vision training typically becomes imbedded in your long-term visual memory. These same-trained skills are reinforced by the visual functioning in everyday life. Tasks such as concentration, reading, driving, and even watching the images on a TV screen or a computer monitor can reinforce these newly developed skills.

◆ *What does it cost?*

Depending on the professional you contract or the facility you use, involved costs can be between $500.00 and $1,200.00.

◆ *Will my insurance cover the fees associated with vision performance training?*

Vision training is typically excluded by most insurance policies, but may be partially covered if carried out by an eyecare practitioner.

◆ *How will I know if I have improved?*

Typically, it is the coach or parent that will be the first to notice the improvement in the athlete's performance. Over extended periods of time you should begin to notice quantifiable improvements (higher batting averages or better fielding of balls, perhaps) and an overall increase of confidence on the field, which can give you a winning edge.

◆ *Where can I find someone with whom to train?*

Information on vision training professionals can be found in the phone book, on web sites and in sports-related journals/magazines. While looking for someone who specializes in the field, try to determine how much of his other time is devoted to this area, as opposed to his regular optometric or ophthalmic duties.

◆ *What do I look for in my players?*

Typically inconsistent play is the first indication of visual skill deficiencies. When players aren't living up to the coaches' expectations, it is probably a good idea to assess the players' visual skills and formulate individualized training programs.

Impact Pyramid

The younger an athlete is when he or she enrolls in a vision performance program, the quicker the result. Older athletes develop compensatory mechanisms to deal with their visual skill deficiencies. A training program typically breaks down these visual *habits* and rebuilds the visual system more accurately and efficiently. Rather than working to break bad habits and develop good ones, as with older athletes, young ball players have an edge. While vision performance training has been used with minor and major league players with great success, Little League is the perfect place to start.

Summary

By their very nature athletes love technology. They're eager to try new products and new techniques. Athletes, coaches and trainers have long recognized the benefits of good nutrition, aerobic conditioning, weight training, and quality equipment. Until recently, however, very few understood the importance of visual skill training. Today no athlete who strives for excellence can ignore the visual system as a vital component of his or her training.

A complete baseball training program should consist of the following elements:

- ♦ Nutrition
- ♦ Weight training
- ♦ Aerobic training
- ♦ Sports psychology
- ♦ Batting and fielding practice
- ♦ Vision performance training

In the end, vision performance training is about correcting deficiencies and enhancing skills that an athlete already has. This type of training offers an edge to athletes – as good as they are, they can always be better, and this might be the key. If you're seeing 20/20 in the doctor's chair, but are 0 for 20 at the plate, it is time to look into a new approach.

Six Exercises You Can Do at Home to Improve Your Visual Skills

The following are some multi-purpose exercises that you can perform at home to improve and enhance your visual skills. Do two or three of these exercises for a total of 30 minutes, three times per week. You may feel some eyestrain, but will not experience pain.

◆ Hold a pencil at arm length. Focus on the pencil's number and move the pencil toward you. When the number begins to blur, extend your arm and begin again. Then hold one pencil in each hand – one as close to your face as possible without the number blurring, and the other at arm length. Focus first on the near pencil (you may notice the distant pencil's blurring into two images). Then stare at the far pencil. Alternate your focus, gradually increasing your speed. Do each exercise for five minutes, rest five minutes and repeat.

◆ Put press-on letters on a Wiffle ball, then hang the ball by a string in a doorway. Twist the string and, while the ball turns, identify as many letters as possible. Perform for three minutes; rest three minutes and repeat.

◆ Place press-on letters or numbers randomly on a clear acetate sheet. Put the acetate over a TV screen. Turn on the TV and try to track the letters or numbers in sequence (a, b, c or 1, 2, 3). Do this for three minutes; rest three minutes and repeat.

◆ While a passenger in a car or while walking briskly, hold your head steady and try to read road signs or license plates on your far right or left, without moving your head or eyes. Do this for five minutes, rest five minutes and repeat.

◆ Turn on a TV station (such as the preview channel) that continuously lists text on the screen. Also open a newspaper. Alternate your reading of the TV and the paper, gradually increasing your speed. Do this for five minutes; rest five minutes and repeat.

◆ To improve your hand-eye-body coordination, perform these exercises while bouncing on a mini-trampoline.

Barry L. Seiller, M.D.

Ophthalmologist
Visual Fitness Institute

Dr. Barry L. Seiller is an ophthalmologist and the founder/director of the Visual Fitness Institute (VFI). Recognizing the interrelated relationship between vision, sports, reading and head injuries, he started VFI in 1989.

Seiller has authored a textbook chapter on head injuries and visual skills, and numerous articles on visual performance training. In 1992 he was chosen as one of three eye doctors who staffed the first Olympic Vision Center in Albertville, France. This led him to accept the position of Director of Visual Performance for the United States Ski and Snowboard Team, and a similar position with the United States Luge and the U.S. Bobsled and Skeleton teams. He became interested in college athletics after designing a program for the University of Texas Baseball Team. This led to the implementation of the Visual Performance Program at the Homer Rice Center on the campus of Georgia Tech for all the student athletes. This is the first of its kind.

In 2002 Seiller was a featured speaker at the American Baseball Coaches Association National Convention and at the Baseball Specific Meeting for the National Strength And Conditioning Coaches Association.

The Institute is now working with the Cleveland Indians and Milwaukee Brewers to identify potential successful players and to improve the skills of minor leaguers.

You can reach Dr. Seiller at 6 Phillip Road, Suite 1110, Vernon Hills, Illinois 60061, by phone at: (847) 816-3131; or at www.visualfitness.com.

CHAPTER 15

Avoiding Slumps: Developing The Mind Of A Champion

Dr. Alan Goldberg
Competitive Advantage

There is absolutely no question that you can't take your talent and game to the next level without first using your head. Far too many talented ball players make the mistake of working very hard on the physical aspects of their game while virtually ignoring the mental part. Sure you have to have good sound throwing, fielding and hitting techniques to excel. Everyone knows that there is no substitute for solid mechanics and good strength and conditioning. However, if you let your training stop there, then you will be seriously limiting your future potential as a ball player. Let me explain.

A colleague of mine who once worked with the California Angels recently described to me what he saw as the primary difference between minor leaguers and those ball players that make it all the way up to the majors. On any given day the minor leaguer has the talent and skills to play in the majors. However, this athlete can't perform at this top level consistently, day in, day out over the course of the season. Why? According to those who know, he is said to lack *maturity*. What is maturity? It's nothing more than mental toughness.

If you don't have the ability to focus on what's important and block out distractions, stay calm under pressure, bust out of slumps, handle self-doubts and negative self-talk or rebound from mistakes and setbacks, which are all component skills of mental toughness, then you'll never be able to fully take your game as far as your dreams. To perform like a champion you must first learn to think like one. In this chapter I'd like to show you how.

Why is it that some ball players always seem to be at their very best in practice but when a game rolls around their skills head South? They hit the ball hard in batting practice, throw nothing but strikes in the bullpen, make great plays in the field and generally look like high caliber athletes. However, in a game situation it is like that movie *Invasion Of The Body Snatchers*. Someone else mysteriously takes over their muscles and game, and suddenly they can't buy a hit, lose the control of and velocity on their pitches, and field as if they have two left feet and stone fingers.

It is the very same reason that some ball players fall into batting and fielding slumps and can't seem to extricate themselves. It all goes back to the kind of mental game you're playing. If you don't have good mental toughness skills, then you will always be more vulnerable to these kinds of performance problems. On the other hand if you do have good, solid mental mechanics, your play will be consistently high and the few slumps you do stumble into won't keep you down for very long.

Step 1 – Developing Awareness

Your first step in developing mental toughness is a very simple one. Before you can strengthen your mental muscles you must first learn to become aware of exactly what you are currently doing mentally that may be getting you into trouble. Specifically you must develop awareness of three key mental areas: 1) Focus of concentration 2) Self-talk 3) Level of pre-performance excitement/nervousness. What you are doing mentally in these three areas will dramatically affect whether you soar with the eagles or gobble with the turkeys. Developing awareness is always the first key step in any kind of positive change regardless of whether you are working on the physical part of your game or the mental one. Let me give you an example.

Billy has been stuck in a nasty batting slump for well over a month. Once the leading hitter on his squad, Billy's batting average and self-confidence have taken a nose-dive, almost completely dropping off the radar screen. No matter what he has tried, he still can't seem to get himself unstuck. In fact, all of his efforts to regain his hitting form have just seemed to backfire, tying him up in knots and making things much worse. Up at the plate Billy presses like crazy. What he doesn't seem to realize is that what he's doing mentally is the real culprit for his hitting problems.

In the on-deck circle Billy's focus of concentration is way off, his self-talk is negative, and both cause him to get too nervous and physically tight to hit well. He thinks about his slump, his low average, what people must be saying about him, and how he needs to get a hit. As he steps up to the plate, the negative chatter intensifies and all he can think about is his plummeting average and what will happen if he doesn't get a hit. As a consequence Billy tries too hard and once again comes up empty.

Busting Billy out of this slump requires that he first become aware of his faulty focus of concentration and negative self-talk. You can't get a hit by concentrating on *needing* to get a hit. You can't get a hit by dwelling on how you haven't been hitting. Success up at the plate can only come when you focus on the important tasks at hand and nothing else. Your batting average, what other people may think about you, needing to knock a run in, or how this at-bat might affect your playing time are far from important. Finally, Billy has to learn to stay calm and loose up at the plate. The secret to consistently hitting the ball hard is being physically relaxed. If you're too excited or too nervous up at the plate because you've made this at-bat too important, if you're trying too hard to get a hit, then your muscles will immediately respond by tightening up. When this happens you can kiss that good at-bat good-bye because it is impossible to hit well when you're uptight.

So how do you go about developing awareness of these three key areas? Spend 10-15 minutes mentally reviewing three or four of your previous good performances. Think back to those times when you were really on as a ball player. Write down what you were thinking about and focusing on right before the game, at-bat or great play that you made. Recall how nervous/excited you were. You should see a common pattern with your focus, self-talk and level of nervousness before your best performances. Next, do the same with several of your bad games. Recall your focus, self-talk and level of physiological arousal right before your bad at-bats or misplays in the field. In a similar way you should see a different kind of pattern with your focus, self-talk and nervousness before your poor performances.

Step 2 – Developing Winning Concentration

The Concentration Difference Between Slumps And Hitting Streaks

Concentration is the key to athletic excellence and the heart of mental toughness. If you want to reach your true potential as a ball player, then you must learn to master this critical mental skill. Your very first step in doing this requires that you understand the major difference between a slump causing and peak-performance focus.

Exhibit I outlines the difference, concentration-wise, between your best performances and your worst, between hitting streaks and slumps. When you struggle as a ballplayer, your focus of concentration both before, and especially during the performance, is what I call, *in your head*. This means that your concentration is predominantly on your thoughts. Simply put, you are *over-thinking* or too conscious. You can be over-thinking mechanical things like what you need to do with your stance, hands, and swing. You can be over-thinking outcome related things like: *What if I don't get a hit? There's a college scout in the stands and I better make sure I play well today.* Or you can be over-thinking negative things like: *I can't believe I missed that throw; what's wrong with me? That pitcher is much too fast for me to hit. You're so bad; you don't even belong on this team.*

There are two main problems with having your *concentration in your head* during the game. First, this thinking focus will distract you from concentrating on the things that will help you play well like the developing play, the ball and the pitcher's release point. Second, over-thinking usually gets you nervous, which immediately leads to tight muscles. When your muscles tighten up, you can kiss your game goodbye because it is impossible to play good ball when you're physically tight.

Another characteristic of this *in your head,* slump-causing focus is that when you walk out onto the field, you're carrying expectations or goals with you. For example, as you loosen up in the on-deck circle you might be thinking about how you need to get a hit, go 3 for 4 to raise your average, or get the runner home to secure your starting position. Expectations are always related to the outcome of the game, play, or at-bat and can also be framed in a negative way. For example, "What if I strike out again" or "What if I let this runner score" are negative expectations. The problem with taking your goals onto the field with you is that you will end up pressuring yourself into trying too hard. Trying too hard is what I call the *game of diminishing returns.* The harder you try, the worse you'll do.

One of Yogi Berra's more famous quotes which captures this *in your head* focus is, "A full mind is an empty bat." That is, if you walk up to the plate with a lot of thoughts crowding your head about needing to get a hit, your average, how good the pitcher is, or what the coach is thinking, then you will come up empty.

When you play your best ball, both offensively and defensively, your focus of concentration during the performance is what I *call in the experience.* When you are *in the experience* your focus is on what you are doing right at that moment and nothing else. Your play is unconscious and thinking does not distract you. Instead, you are concentrating on those little physical and visual cues that are necessary in order for you to execute your very best. For example, a hitter up at the plate may be focusing only on staying loose, the pitcher's release point and seeing the ball. A pitcher may be focusing on just the target and the feeling of the ball in his hand.

Exhibit # 1

CONCENTRATION	
CHOKING/SLUMPS	**PEAK PERFORMANCE**
In Your Head	In the Experience (Game)
Over-Thinking	No Thinking
Focus on Thoughts	Focus on Seeing/Feeling/Doing
Tight Muscles	Loose Muscles
Expectations	No Expectations

When your focus is in the experience of the game you will always stay physically and mentally relaxed. In addition, you will approach the game, play, or at-bat with absolutely no expectations. You play as if you have nothing to lose, without worry about the game's outcome, needing to drive this runner home or how this at-bat will affect your batting average. As a consequence of this, you get into what I call *a trust and let it happen* headset. You trust your training and skills, and you just let the performance happen.

It is only when your concentration is in the right column that you will be able to play at your very best. It is only in the right column that you will be able to bust out of that hitting slump. As you approach a game, you need to learn to discipline yourself to shift your focus to the right column. How do you do this?

The Mechanics Of Winning Concentration

Concentration is the heart of mental toughness and the secret to playing your best under pressure. Very simply, concentration is the ability to focus on what is *important* and block out *everything else*. Without this ability all the good coaching that you have had, all the hard work you have invested, and all your natural talent will be wasted. Baseball players who struggle with slumps and other repetitive performance problems do so mainly because they haven't yet learned to control their focus of concentration.

So how do you know what's *really* important at any given time during a game? There are two things that are critical for you to consider when we talk about what's important concentration-wise. These are the two dimensions of concentration: time; and place.

The Time Dimension

Whenever you perform, whether in a game situation or practice, your focus of concentration can be in one of three mental time zones: The Past; The Present or Now; and The Future. When you are thinking about an error after you committed it, your last at-bat, what happened the last time you faced this pitcher, how you lost to this same team earlier in the season, how you haven't hit in your last five games, then your focus is in the past. Similarly, when you are thinking about needing to get a hit, worrying about the *what ifs,* (What if I strike out? What if I drop the ball? What if I get benched? What if we lose?), then your concentration is in the future.

When you keep your focus on what you are doing, *while* you are doing it you are said to be in the *now.* The only way that you can accomplish this is to take each game one pitch/play at a time and each at-bat, one ball at a time. Staying in the *now* is the most critical mental task for you as a ball player. Why? Simple! The only mental time zone that you have access to your skills is the *now.* The only time zone that you're going to get a hit in or make that great play in is the *now.* You will not be able to take your game to the next level without first developing the ability to stay in the *now* whenever you play.

One of the biggest mental mistakes made by ball players at *every* level and the one that is most responsible for hitting and fielding slumps is what I call time traveling. The ball player mentally goes from the past to the future and back again while the game is going on instead of staying in the now. For example, the struggling batter will be in the on-deck circle worrying about his last several bad at-bats, (the past). Then he will jump into the future and start thinking about how he needs to get a hit (the future) and worries *what if* he doesn't (the future). It's this mental time traveling from the past to the future that tightens the athlete physically, distracts him from the task at hand, and sets him up to fail once again.

Concentration's Place Dimension

Just as there's a proper mental time zone where you need to focus, so too there's a proper mental place. Far too many ball players are mentally in the wrong place whenever they field or bat. For example, the college ball player who is up at the plate yet thinking about the pro scouts watching is in the wrong mental place. Mentally he is sitting in the stands right next to those scouts. The pitcher who is upset with and focuses on what he considers to be the umpire's continually changing strike zone and bad calls is also mentally in the wrong place. Instead of being on the mound, mentally he is behind the plate with the umpire. Similarly, the short stop who keeps thinking that the coach is going to bench him for a recent error is no longer on the field mentally, but in the dugout with the coach.

In order to play your very best you have to train yourself to keep your focus in the right mental place, on what you are doing at that moment. This means that you have to learn to stay in the *here*. Disciplining yourself to stay in the right mental place and focusing on what you are doing will prevent you from getting psyched out or intimidated.

The Mental Muscle of Concentration

So how do you learn to develop this master skill of mental toughness? Quite simply! You just need to know how to concentrate. Concentration is what is called a paradoxical skill. That is, you learn to concentrate by catching yourself when you're not concentrating. First, you have to immediately recognize the instant that your focus of concentration leaves what is important. Second, you have to quickly and gently return your focus back to what is important.

For example, you have to immediately recognize that you are focusing on the last play and the error you just committed, and then you have to quickly bring yourself back to the *now* and the present play. You have to catch yourself whenever you start focusing on the coach and what he may be thinking about you, and then quickly return your focus to what is going on at your position. You have to be aware that you are thinking too much about getting a hit, and bring your focus back to staying calm, picking up the pitcher's release point, and seeing the ball.

The key to mental toughness is this recognition and return skill. Keep in mind that a break in concentration won't really hurt you as a ball player. What will hurt you big time is a break in concentration that you don't immediately catch and return from. If you can train yourself to be on top of your mental drifting and quickly bring yourself back whenever it happens, then you will soon find that the level of your play becomes higher and more consistent.

Use the following homework exercise to strengthen your concentration muscles.

Take a ball and place it three or four feet away from you. Pick a spot on the ball where you can gently rest your eyes. Sitting comfortably and looking at your spot, put the rest of your concentration on the feeling of your inhalation, breathing normally. When you exhale, repeat the word ball to yourself. Inhale; focus on the feeling of the breath coming in; exhale; and focus on ball. Remember your eyes will stay on your spot the entire time. Since watching a stationary ball is unbelievably boring, you will probably notice that as you do this, your focus will periodically drift. If that happens, immediately recognize that you have lost your focus, and then quickly bring your concentration back to the spot, your breathing and the word *ball*.

Spend three minutes a day doing this part of the exercise without any distractions. Then take your ball, place it on top of a TV set, turn the TV on and then sit far enough away from the set so that in order to see your spot, you have to see the entire TV screen. Now try to continue the same exercise without getting distracted by what's on the TV. Whenever you find yourself distracted, catch yourself right away and then quickly come back to the ball, your breathing and your cue word.

Step 3 – Training Your Inner Coach

Mastering Negative Thinking And Self-doubts

Your mind can be an unbelievably powerful positive or negative force in affecting your performance. What you think or say to yourself before or during an at-bat or play will make or break how well you perform. If you don't have control over this pre-performance self-talk, then you will never be able to reach your full potential as a ballplayer.

All too often an athlete will step up to the plate in a pressure packed situation and a flood of last minute negative thinking and self-doubts will suddenly wash over him. *What if I strike out and leave the runners stranded? Then we'll lose and it'll be my fault. You've got to get a hit. Last time you were in this position you hit a weak grounder to second base. You always mess up when it counts the most. Don't blow it now!*

If you allow yourself to listen to this self-confidence eroding chatter, then you will end up getting emotionally hijacked. Your emotions will run away with your skills leaving you tied up in knots and performing badly.

Is there anything that you can do to prevent this from happening? Absolutely! One of the master skills of mental toughness is having the ability to effectively handle this last minute negativity and self-doubt. Here's how.

First you must understand that negative thinking and last minute self-doubts are normal. Even the very best ball players in the major leagues have them going on in their heads at one time or another right before a big game or crucial at-bat.

Second, even though you have negative thinking going on in your head, you can still play out of your mind as long as you deal with these negative thoughts the right way. Whenever you hear that negative tape playing in your head, your primary job is to use the negative thinking and self-doubts as a neutral signal to relax and refocus.

Far too many ball players panic at the very first sound of this internal negativity. They begin to listen to the dialogue and get too caught up in the actual content of the words. The skill you need to adopt here is to not jump into the content of the negative self-talk and instead to instantly refocus yourself on the task at hand. Negative thinking will only hurt your performance if you engage it. You hear the words and begin to battle with them in your head. When you do this you will not only distract your concentration from the game, but you'll also tighten yourself up and undermine your self-confidence.

Imagine hearing your negative thoughts and doubts in a language that you don't understand. If your favorite negative phrases played in your head in Russian, for example, what would you actually hear? Gibberish. Why? You wouldn't be able to understand the meaning of the words. This is the way that you want to approach those old familiar negative tapes that sometimes play in your mind. You don't have to stop them completely. That is really not necessary. Instead, you must train yourself to respond calmly to them by quickly refocusing yourself on whatever is going on in the game at that moment. If you find that the negative thoughts return within 15 seconds, quickly refocus yourself again and as many times as necessary over the course of the game.

Let me give you an example. Let's say I'm pitching in a huge game and there are college scouts in the stands. It is in the bottom of the fifth, I have a two-run lead but there are runners on the corners and I only have one out. On top of all this I'm behind in the count, 3 and 1. Naturally in a stressful situation like this my friendly negative thoughts and self-doubts will stop by for a visit to offer some helpful insight. *What if I walk this guy? Then I'll have bases loaded. But if I throw to him he could hit me. I know he's a good hitter. Last week he hit a game winning home run off of Oakdale's pitcher and that guy was supposed to be good! That's all I need right now and especially with those State coaches in the stands. I'm going to blow it! I can just feel it.*

Now the very worst thing for me to do when I hear this negative inner chatter is to jump in to the content and start fighting with it. For example, *I've got to really bear down here so I throw well. I've got to strike this guy out. I can do it. I've got to do it! A scholarship is riding in the balance here. Let's go! Come on!* By jumping in and engaging with my negative thoughts in this way I will end up physically tightening up and trying too hard.

So instead I will respond to myself with a little humor and then use the doubts and negative thoughts as nothing more than a signal to refocus. First I step off the mound and then think to myself: *I seem to be in the middle of a baseball game here. Perhaps you'd like to get yourself a beverage and a hot dog while you're waiting.* Then I leave the humor and start coaching myself in a positive way: *O.K. Relax.... Breathe.... Just one pitch at a time. Just this pitch. Nothing else. Stay in the now.* After reassuring myself in this way, which incidentally should take no more than a few seconds, I will then return my concentration to my target and my pre-pitch ritual.

Keep in mind that negative thinking is nothing more than brain wave activity. It won't knock you off balance and upset you unless you let it. Know that it's normal. Know that you don't have to stop the negative thinking completely. Relax when you hear it and then quickly and calmly return your focus to the *now* and the important task at hand.

Step 4 – Avoid The Ball Player's Biggest Mental Trap

Focusing On The UCs

One of the biggest mental mistakes made by ball players at every level is also one of the most costly performance-wise. This mistake is responsible for athletes' choking and getting stuck in slumps. The athlete who consistently makes this mental error always suffers from out-of-control nervousness and low self-confidence. The mistake I'm referring to is a concentration one and is outlined in Exhibit #2.

Exhibit #2

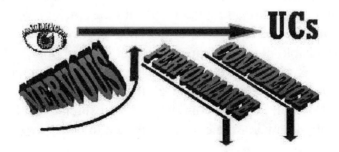

When you go into a game, (at-bat or defensive play) and you focus on a class of things I call the UCs (the uncontrollables), three things will almost always happen to you. First, your stress level will go up which will lead to increased nervousness and tighter muscles. Second, your self-confidence will go down. Third, as a result of these first two, your performance will rapidly head down the tubes.

The uncontrollables are all those things in your sport that are directly out of your control. Some common UCs are: everything about your opponent (size, strength, talent, reputation, style of play); the weather; playing and field conditions; the umpires and their calls; the fans and size of the crowd; the play and behavior of your team-mates; your playing time; the coaches; time of the game; an error or anything in the past; the outcome of the game or anything in the future; how you feel that day; injuries; other people's expectations of you and what the media writes.

How do you handle the UCs? You have to learn to do two things whenever you're confronted by an uncontrollable: First, you must immediately recognize the instant that your focus goes to an uncon-trollable. Second, you have to quickly and gently return your con-centration back to the game and what you *can* control at that moment. Understand that focusing on an uncontrollable by itself won't hurt you. What will hurt you is when you focus on that uncontrollable and fail to return your focus right away. It's when you allow the UCs to have extended *airplay* in your head that you will end up getting into hot water performance-wise.

Keep in mind that the UCs are mental traps. The bigger the game, the more vulnerable you will be to stumbling into these traps. The only way for you to avoid them is to know what they are. It's your awareness and avoidance of the uncontrollables that will keep you calm and confident under pressure. To help you get good at iden-tifying and therefore avoiding these mental traps, make a written list of all the UCs that have previously bothered you. Next, post the list in a highly visible place, perhaps over your desk in your bedroom. Be sure to look at this list every day, especially before practice and games. Remind yourself, as you do so, that each of these uncontrol-lables is out of your control! This simple little exercise will help you to get to really know your uncontrollables and to better avoid them.

Step 5 – Stay Loose And Relaxed

The secret to consistently playing your best when the heat of competition is turned way up high is such a simple skill that most athletes frequently overlook it. If you learn to master this skill, you will have developed one of the primary keys to mental toughness. If you really want to take your game to the next level, this mental toughness skill will help you get there.

What I am referring to here is the simple skill of relaxation, of staying loose under pressure. If you do not know how to relax going into a crucial game, at-bat or defensive play, then you'll consistently under-achieve. Staying physically and mentally relaxed just before and during your performances is a critical prerequisite for peak performance. Choking, slumps and just about all performance problems in this game are a direct result of being too nervous right before or during execution.

If you make a game or at-bat too important, if you put too much pressure on yourself to *produce* or *not mess up*, then your muscles will respond by immediately tightening which, in turn, will sabotage your efforts and dramatically undermine your best performance. Instead you want to train yourself to make staying loose and relaxed a priority before you play. The bigger the game, the more important relaxing becomes. The better you want to play, the more you need to focus all your energies on staying calm.

How do you do this?

Probably one of the fastest and easiest ways to calm yourself down and get back in control whenever you're under pressure is by deliberately slowing and deepening your breathing. When an athlete begins to get nervous his breathing instantly becomes faster and shallower. It's this faster, shallower breathing that will ultimately tighten you up more, increase your nervousness and lead to a bad performance. By slowing down and deepening your breathing whenever you start feeling nervous, you will quickly regain your composure. Practicing the following exercise will help you develop confidence in your ability to stay calm under pressure:

Sit comfortably in an environment free from distractions. Close your eyes and put your entire focus of concentration on your diaphragm or lower belly. Inhale through your nose to a slow count of four, feeling your diaphragm filling up completely. Pause briefly and then exhale slowly to a little faster count of seven or eight. Repeat the process being sure to keep your entire focus of concentration on your diaphragms rising and falling. If you find your focus drifting, quickly return it to your breathing. Spend three to four minutes a day with this exercise. Keep in mind that shorter, more frequent practice sessions are far more valuable than longer, less frequent sessions.

With consistent practice of this exercise, you will notice that just one or two of these diaphragmatic breaths will quickly calm you down whenever you find yourself in a tight situation.

Summary

Keep in mind that if you're serious about your baseball, then you must start today to work on developing your mental muscles. You will never reach your potential as a ball player if you leave the mental side of your game to chance. To become a champion you must take the time to systematically develop the mind of a champion.

Practice These Six Steps To Mental Toughness:

1) Develop awareness of your pre-and during-game thoughts and focus.
2) Learn to properly concentrate by staying in the *here and the now.*
3) Develop the discipline to immediately recognize when you lose your focus and then quickly bring yourself back.
4) Stay calm when you hear internal negative chatter and use this negative self-talk as a signal to relax and refocus on the task at hand.
5) Know what your uncontrollables are and do not let them have any *airtime* in your head.
6) Finally, learn to stay calm and relax under pressure.

Dr. Alan Goldberg

Competitive Advantage
Amherst, Massachusetts

Alan S. Goldberg, Ed.D., is the director of *Competitive Advantage,* a sports consulting firm in Amherst, Massachusetts. A practicing sports psychology consultant since 1983, he has worked with hundreds of coaches and slumping athletes and teams across a wide variety of sports, competition levels, and ages. Dr. Goldberg was on staff at the University of Connecticut as the Huskies' sports psychologist and worked with the 1998 NCAA Men's National Basketball Championship team, the 2000 NCAA Women's National Basketball Championship team, and the 2000 NCAA Men's National Soccer Champions. Dr. Goldberg has gained a unique perspective on developing mental toughness as a professional tennis instructor for more than 22 years and as a former number one singles player and twice conference champion as a student at the University of Massachusetts.

Dr. Goldberg is a nationally known expert in the field of applied sports psychology and maintains both an extensive speaking schedule and private practice, specializing in helping slumping athletes get unstuck and back on track. He is the author of *Sports Slump Busting, Playing Out of Your Mind,* five mental toughness workbooks and twelve audiocassette/CD mental toughness-training programs. In addition to working with amateur and professional athletes and coaches, Dr. Goldberg is a regular presenter at the U.S. Olympic Training Center in Colorado Springs.

Dr. Goldberg lives in Amherst, Massachusetts, with his wife, Renee, and two daughters, Sara and Julee. He enjoys karate, tennis, the beach, and sports with his children.

To reach Dr. Goldberg, call 413-549-1085 or fax him at 413-549-4196. E-mail is IbustSlump@aol.com You can also order his best-selling tapes at www.competitivedge.com.

CHAPTER 16

Mental Toughness: Five Steps To Consistent Confidence

Tom Hanson, Ph.D.
Personal and Professional Coach

What percentage of your performance on a given day would you say is determined by *mental game* factors such as your confidence, focus, and motivation?

The answer I most often receive from the players I speak with is around 80%. But when I ask them what percentage of their time they spend working on their mental game, they typically say 0-20%. It isn't that players and coaches don't know the mental game is vital – they agree it is the most important part of the game. The problem is they don't know how to develop it or don't make the time for it. My mission is to close the gap between the importance of the mental game and the attention it receives. I'm committed to helping players play better and enjoy the game more.

Funda-Mentals

I define mental toughness as the ability to consistently play at or near your best regardless of circumstances. That means no matter what situation you are in, regardless of what has happened in the past, or what might happen in the future, you are able to play nearly as well as you are capable of playing.

Anyone can play great when they feel great, but players who succeed at the higher levels are able to create good or even great performances when they don't feel 100%. They might be tired or frustrated, or they might have doubts about their ability to succeed (doubt happens to the best of players, even at the major league level), but somehow they are able to focus the energy they do have in a way that produces success.

How Do They Do It?

In this chapter I offer what I've learned from some of the best players in the history of the game about how to consistently play at or near your best. Of course, knowledge alone will do you no good, nor will trying it once. You need to put your knowledge into repeated, consistent action, so I'll give you some ideas on how to do that.

Being confident is a choice you make. Sometimes it is a choice you can make in an instant, which allows you to shift quickly from doubt to belief. The ideas discussed in this chapter will help you learn to be better at shifting from doubt to belief. But most of the time it is like choosing to add 25 pounds to your maximum bench press: You choose to take the necessary steps that get you there over time.

The *there* you are trying to get to is being able to generate the feeling or *state* that allows you to play great. Although I'm sure at times you've gotten good results when you didn't feel confident, most of your best performances come when you believe and feel you are going to be successful.

Here's a great quote that sums it up from one of the mentally toughest athletes ever, Michael Jordan.

"What happens to clutch guys in big moments is that everything slows down. You have time to evaluate the situation,
and you can clearly see every move you need to make.
You're in the moment, in complete control. It's hard to get
there; something has to have you thinking you can do no
wrong. But once you do get there, you can just come out at
the start of a game and generate the feeling."

(Williams & Weinreb, 2001, p. 1)

The key to your success is your ability to learn to *generate the
feeling*. Another way to say it is to *manage your state*, or *control the
way you focus and feel*. It is your ability to create the feeling of confidence, or at least direct your focus and energy in such a way that
you are able to let your talent come through.

I believe that your natural state is to be and play great. Think
about it; when you were a kid playing whiffle-ball in the backyard or
street, did guys *choke?* Usually not. When you are playing out of
shear love of the game the way kids do, you usually play very well.

But as you get older, things get in the way. Because you think
more and have had more life experience, you likely find it harder to
play with the same sense of freedom, fun and abandon you did when
you were younger. As your brain develops you have a greater
tendency to think when you should just *do*.

You may have been one of those guys whose feet grew faster
than the rest of his body and you routinely tripped over yourself.
Your mind is the same way. As it develops it is able to better serve
you in many ways, but it also becomes more likely to get in your
way! You can see guys tripping over their own brain at most high
school, college and professional games.

The key is to get your mind working *for* you, not against you.
How you think and what you pay attention to dictate your performance. Top players habitually think thoughts and focus on things that
help their performance. Lesser players have less effective thinking
habits.

One of the advantages of having a human brain is the ability to
choose your thoughts and focus. Although it usually doesn't seem
like it, we are all making choices throughout each day about what we

think and what we focus on. Since what we think about and focus on are so critical to performance, the key is to make good choices with your thoughts, and focus until the helpful ones become habits. It is no different from learning a new pitch or new footwork for a backhand. You create a new image of what you want, then you practice it until it becomes habit.

Very few people are committed enough to make profound changes in how they think. It is not easy.

Most players ride the *Results Roller Coaster* – when they are successful and getting good results, they feel confident and think positively, but when they fail they free-fall into doubt and negativity. I enjoy roller coasters at theme parks, but not at ballparks. Think about it: Once you get on a roller coaster at a theme park you have no control over where you go. You just hang on and go for a ride.

My purpose is to help you put your hands on the controls of your performance. I want you to drive rather than be taken for a ride. My mission is to provide you with the knowledge and structure you need to consistently make great choices with what you focus on and what actions you take. Only by applying yourself fully to the mental game can you retire from the game knowing you did everything you could with the ability you were given.

Rising Above Your Circumstances

It is said that baseball is a game of failure. As you experience more and more failure, it often becomes harder to maintain the confident, even cocky mindset you probably had as a kid. I said I define mental toughness as the ability to consistently play at or near your best regardless of circumstances. You may start out a day or a game feeling good, but then something happens that gets in the way of your being your natural, confident self.

I call it being *hooked.* You are going along fine and then something grabs your attention and it pulls you off course. Your mind bites on it like a fish on a hook and you get upset, frustrated, angry, or scared and your performance suffers. You can get hooked by external circumstances (things outside you) or internal circumstances (things inside you).

External Circumstances

Scouts and College Coaches - One of your biggest *hooks* can be having scouts and college coaches in the stands. Many players have a hard time staying focused on what is most important (the game) when they want so badly to impress the scouts. It is hard for your body to play well when your head is in the stands.

School - Schoolwork can be a major distraction. If you are behind in school, it drains your energy and hurts your baseball performance because part of your mind is occupied with what needs to be done. You can't be 100% focused on baseball when part of your brain is concerned about school. You might not be aware of the loss of focus and energy caused by being behind or doing poorly, but it is like a slow leak in your car tire. You're losing air whether you know it or not.

Relationships - Relationship issues, especially with girlfriends, distract players at all levels. But at least as many have their performance enhanced by a great relationship. The issue isn't whether you have or don't have a relationship; it is how you are being in the relationship. Like with your schoolwork, integrity is key. If you are truthful, respectful, and do what you say you are going to do, chances are the relationship will help your game. But if you aren't acting with integrity, there is a good chance your relationship will be distracting to your performance.

Your Coach - Coaches often make unpopular decisions. Even if you respect your coach, you are apt to disagree with him at some point. Many players, not getting the playing time they want, focus on how unfair or disappointing it is, and it robs them of the positive energy they need to play well when they do get a chance to play.

Your Statistics - Many players obsess over their statistics. I've known pitchers to be on the mound calculating their ERA during the middle of an inning (*If this guy scores, that will be three earned runs in five innings so that means...*), and hitters pressuring themselves when they are 0 for 3. Instead of being focused on what they need to do to have a great at bat, they are focused on not being 0 for 4. It is a pretty selfish approach since you are totally focused on you instead of your team, and it distracts you from focusing on how you can help your team on the next pitch. Your statistics won't get you a scholarship. If they did, scouts and coaches wouldn't bother coming to the games.

Success - Success is one of the most dangerous and seductive obstacles. A pitcher on the mound might think: *I'm really doing great. I'm just five outs away from getting my ERA under 3.00 again.* Next thing you know the guy doesn't make it out of the inning he's in because he's not focused on what he's doing. Sometimes the worst thing that can happen to you as a hitter is to hit a home run. You start thinking about hitting more of them, and it may take you weeks to recover and get back to being yourself.

Other external circumstances that can disrupt your focus include:
- Bad calls by umpires.
- Off-the-field issues such as alcohol, drugs, and money.
- Teammates.
- Weather.
- Field conditions.
- Your opponent being really good or really bad.
- Fans.
- Media.
- Travel.

Internal circumstances (things going on inside you) that can hook you include:
- Fear.
- Anger.
- Frustration.
- Fatigue.
- Negative thoughts.

Ultimately, getting hooked is always the result of an internal process. Something happens and you make it mean something that upsets you or scares you. You think something like, *That shouldn't happen. That's not fair. Why does bad stuff always happen to me?* and you're hooked! Your body gets tense and you are no longer focused on baseball; now you're focused on the thing that upset you.

When you strike out you're just out. That's it. Nowhere in the rulebook does it say you should be upset about it or that the next time up you should swing as hard as you can so you can make up for the strike out! Your emotion about the whole thing results from your thinking, not the event itself.

As William Shakespeare (who would have been a great baseball writer) said, "Nothing is neither good nor bad, but thinking makes it so."

Imagine it is the fourth inning, there are two outs, a man on first, and Charlie is at the plate. After taking a fastball high for ball one Charlie hits a line drive, but it is right at the short stop who catches the ball without taking a single step. The inning is over, and Charlie is out. While the players on both sides hustle in and hustle out, Charlie is flooded with thoughts and feelings.

How do you think Charlie will react to this situation?

1. He'll be upset, angry, and think, *I'll never get another hit.*
2. He'll be disappointed, but okay. Knowing he saw the ball well and hit it on the nose, he'll think, *Wow, I can't wait to hit again.*
3. It depends.

If you chose number three, you'd make a good sport psychologist. That is the way they always respond to questions. Yes, it depends. It depends on how Charlie sees the situation, what kind of mood he's in, how things have been going for him lately, and what he chooses to focus on. The more confident he is, the more likely he will respond as in number 2.

Here are five strategies to help you build and maintain your confidence, regardless of your circumstances: Move Confidently, Think Confidently, Focus Confidently, Prepare Confidently, and Remember Why You Play Baseball.

> **Five Steps to Consistent Confidence**
> 1. **Move Confidently**
> 2. **Think Confidently**
> 3. **Focus Confidently**
> 4. **Prepare Confidently**
> 5. **Remember Why You Play Baseball**

Confidence Strategy # 1

Move Confidently

When you are playing great, how do you carry yourself between pitches?

The fastest and easiest route to becoming more confident is to move your body confidently. How do you move when you feel totally unstoppable? Try it right now. Stand up and walk around the room like you feel totally confident. Lift your head up high, let your shoulders roll back, raise your chin and chest and draw full, slow breaths deep into your abdomen. Now get into your batting stance or stand on an imaginary pitching rubber like you're certain you are the best, like you are in complete control of the situation. How does that feel? (Chances are you didn't do it. Come on and give it a try!)

When your body is moving confidently, it sends messages to your brain that you are confident. It feels good to move that way, so you start to think more confident thoughts. It is very difficult to think confidently when you body is in a slumped position, and very easy to think confidently when your body is standing tall and broad.

Pretend you are back in a time when you dominated, when you felt really great. You don't have to make a big show of it, just move confidently. You may also want to try doing an impression of a confident-looking major league player that you like. Don't just try to think your way to a new level of moving, *move* your way to a new level of thinking!

Confidence Strategy # 2
Think Confidently

When you are playing great, what do you spend your time thinking about? I'll bet when you are playing well that you spend your time thinking about playing well. Between games you can't wait to get to the park again because your head is filled with images and feelings of yourself playing great.

Similarly, when you are slumping, I'll bet you spend your time thinking about playing poorly. Between games you almost dread going to the park because your body is filled with thoughts, images and feelings of playing poorly. It is like you have an obnoxious fan for the other team inside your head riding you relentlessly telling you how horrible you are. Not exactly a recipe for success.

Think in a way that gives you the best chance for success regardless of your circumstances. When you are 0 for 7 or just gave up a three run homer to tie the game, you still are able to choose your thoughts. You can think: *I'm due! I'm the best man for this situation and I'm going to get the job done right now.*

Choose to think confident thoughts enough and it becomes a habit. Great players habitually think in ways that help their performance. Some great players are very hard on themselves mentally, but when it comes time to perform they get their minds out of the way enough to get the job done.

It sounds simple, but not many players choose to spend their time thinking about playing great. And don't just think it; feel it in your body as you picture it in your mind. This becomes a habit, the way you learn any physical skill – through focused repetitions.

Confidence Strategy # 3
Focus Confidently

Your performance follows your focus. Imagine you are riding a bike and you stare off to the left for a few seconds. Where is your bike now going? To the left! You might think you're staying straight, you might intend to stay straight, but your body and your performance will follow your focus.

Your success is determined by your ability to have a focused connection with your target regardless of circumstances: For pitchers, it is the mitt; for hitters and fielders, it is the ball. So, what should you focus on? The first answer is for you to recall what you focus on when you are playing your best.

I asked a pitcher (who as a rookie succeeded over many other excellent pitchers in winning a starting position on a major league team) how he had done it. "I shrunk the game," he said, meaning instead of getting caught up in the many distractions that come with major league baseball, including the media and playing with and against players he had grown up admiring, he chose to focus on a few simple things.

There are three basic elements to shrinking the game. If you are struggling in your performance you are probably not doing at least one of them.

1) Focus on things you can control. What can you control? Your playing time? The outcome of the game? Getting a base hit? Getting a batter out? Getting a college scholarship?

No, you can't actually control any of these things. You care deeply about them, and you can influence them, but you can't control them. Don't waste your energy or base your confidence solely on any of them. Focus on your thinking, your attitude, your effort, the quality of your practice, and the quality of your preparation. Focus on the process of playing the game instead of being wrapped up in your results.

Former NCAA Division I Coach of the Year, Dave Snow says, "Results thinking is just a big trap. You've got to work on your physical and mental skills and then go out, trust what you've worked on and accept the results."

2) Focus on the present moment. The second step to *shrinking the game* relates closely to the first because the only time you have any control is right now. You can't change the past, you can't do anything about the future (it is in the future). Regardless of what happened on the last pitch (your circumstances) or what might happen on some later pitch, the only pitch that you can do anything about is this next one. Focus on it.

Play the game *one pitch at a time*. Hopefully, you've heard this saying many times, but it is doubtful you're really great at doing it. Pitchers in the major leagues struggle to do it. It is very difficult to stay fully focused on this one pitch and not be negatively affected by anything that's happened on a previous pitch.

3) Focus on the most important thing. The final step in shrinking the game is to figure out the most important thing. For pitchers it is the mitt (or whatever you are using for a target). For hitters it is the ball. For fielders it is the ball and then your target for your throw.

It's great to know what to focus on, but being able to focus consistently is a skill you develop with practice. I've learned many ways to develop your ability to focus, but the simplest is just to commit yourself to being fully focused on things you can control, in the present moment, that are most important – and then go out and do it. When you get *hooked* and lose your focus, re-focus.

Confidence Strategy # 4
Prepare Confidently
Several years ago I interviewed Hank Aaron, the all-time leader in runs batted in, total bases, and home runs. I asked him about the mental aspects of hitting, and his first words were, "Well, it all depends on how a guy prepares himself to do battle." He attributed his incredible consistency and ability to perform under pressure to his ability to focus. His tremendous focus, he said, resulted from his daily mental preparation.

Similarly I recently interviewed Ferguson Jenkins. Once I asked about the mental aspects of pitching, the entire rest of the interview was about mental preparation. He spoke about going through the opposing team's line-up in his head not only before the game, but also between each inning. He'd prepare while his team was hitting by thinking through the first four hitters of the next inning.

By the way, pretty much all of my good information on how to be great mentally comes from great players. My approach throughout my career has been to interview people who are among the best at what they do and make that information available to others.

Preparation is one of the most powerful sources of confidence. Aren't you more confidant going into an exam at school if you've studied thoroughly than if you haven't? A baseball game is no different. The better you've done your homework studying your opponent and preparing your mind and body to play, the more confident you're likely to be.

To help with this process, I've devised a mental preparation strategy called P.R.E.P. that gives you a systematic way to approach this key source of confidence. I take you through the whole process in my online mental toughness training course, but in this chapter I'll limit it to the last letter *P*.

The last *P* stands for *Pre-play Your Performance*. Use your imagination to see, feel and hear the way you want the game to go. Aaron told me he prepared by visualizing himself facing the pitcher he would see that night. He saw each of the pitchers' pitches coming in, and he put himself in different game situations.

You can do the same thing and probably do to some extent already. Put yourself in different situations, imagine throwing great pitches or hitting the ball on the nose time after time. You can do it throughout the day of your practice or game, or set aside 5-10 minutes to really focus in on it. Be sure to feel it, and even hear the action, not just see it. Don't worry if your images aren't perfectly clear; just get into it. You must be focused to pre-play, and doing it will get you mentally and emotionally prepared to play.

Confidence Strategy # 5
Remember Why You Play

It is great if your goal is to get a college scholarship. College baseball is one of the best experiences out there. But don't lose sight of why you play baseball in the first place. Did you start playing as a kid so you could get a college scholarship? Of course not. So don't fall into the trap of thinking every game you play now is about your getting onto the college team you want to play for.

Play with the love of the game, the passion, the joy, and the fun that you had as a child – even if your coach or some other circumstance is making that difficult. College will come soon enough. Savor every moment of high school baseball, or a few years from now you'll look back and wish you had!

Structures Of Support

None of these ideas are of any value unless you apply them. They each have the ability to increase your confidence in an instant, helping you generate *the feeling* Jordan spoke of earlier. Psychologists estimate a new habit takes 21 to 30 days to develop. Hitters who lunge or have a long swing, and pitchers who drift or fly open know that change rarely happens over night. That's why it is so important that you get some assistance in implementing these ideas.

The final element in making a change is creating a structure to support you. A structure is something that reminds you, if not forces you, to stick to your plan. It keeps you from getting fired up about something for a moment or a few days, then forgetting about it when you don't feel so fired up about it later.

Daily baseball practice is a structure. You have a set time and place where you practice your skills. How good would your team be if everyone only practiced when he felt like it?

Other examples of structures include:
a) progress charts (often used in weight training).
b) a partner (like a workout buddy).
c) a coach.
d) a class.

Without a structure that holds you accountable, you usually start strong, but then forget about your commitment. Since your new skill is not yet ingrained, circumstances will distract you and your focus will shift to something else, leaving you with your old behavior. People who want to lose weight and don't, usually fail because they don't put proper structures in place to support them. Willpower alone rarely works.

If in two weeks the information in this chapter has not noticeably enhanced your confidence, you are lacking in effective structure of support. For more information about how to more effectively implement the ideas in this chapter, see *www.FocusedBaseball.com*, or write to me at *Tom@FocusedBaseball.com*.

Summary

The foundation of mental toughness lies in your taking responsibility for your own thinking. Instead of riding the *results roller coaster* where your thinking is determined solely by your statistics and how you happen to feel, you deliberately choose to think in ways that give you your best chance to succeed. Like Michael Jordan, you learn to generate confident feelings rather than just hoping you feel good.

You are naturally confident, but many things distract you from playing that way. Some happen during a game, some may have happened years ago. Regardless, external and internal events will conspire to hook you, undermining your confidence and disrupting your focus.

I discussed five choices you can make to build your confidence: Move Confidently, Think Confidently, Focus Confidently, Prepare Confidently, and Remember Why You Play. But your best intentions of building and solidifying your confidence will likely fail unless you put some structure in place that supports you in your learning. Baseball is such a humbling game that it can undermine the confidence of the most self-assured player unless he gets some help from somewhere.

One of the characteristics of successful teams is they serve as a structure of support for each team member to be confident. Don't just hope that happens on your team, be a leader and choose to generate a confidence-building environment.

Tom Hanson, Ph.D.

Personal and Professional Coach
Tampa, Florida

Tom Hanson has coached baseball players ranging from the world champions to little leaguers since 1983.

Tom began his career by playing high school baseball in Moorhead, Minnesota. He then played college ball at Luther College. He served as a graduate assistant at the University of Illinois, the hitting coach at The University of Virginia, and head coach at Skidmore College in New York. He has also coached youth sport teams and directed sports camps and clinics.

He received his M.S. in Sports Psychology in 1987, his Ph.D. in Sports Psychology in 1991, and became a Certified Personal and Professional Coach in 2000. Recently he has performed services for the Anaheim Angels and Minnesota Twins to promote performance enhancement, he has acted as a Performance Enhancement Consultant for the Texas Rangers, and in 2001 was the full-time Performance Enhancement Director for the New York Yankees.

Tom has coached and trained business people and organizations ranging from Fortune 500 companies to start-ups, and has held interviews with sport greats such as Nolan Ryan, Tommy John, Ferguson Jenkins, Bert Blyleven, Hank Aaron, Rod Carew, Pete Rose, Tony Olivia, Carl Yastrzemski, Stan Musial, Kirby Puckett, Billy Williams and many other current major league players.

He is the co-author of *Heads-Up Baseball: Playing the Game One Pitch at a Time*, and has a vision to establish a *virtual university* where anyone can take classes, read, and listen to information on enhancing their performance and the enjoyment of the game of baseball.

Visit his web-site, *www.FocusedBaseball.com*, and sign up for his free newsletter. He also has an online Mental Toughness Program that is available for one-on-one mental toughness lessons on the phone.

You can reach Tom at: Heads-Up Performance Inc., 8639 North Himes Avenue #2224, Tampa, FL 33614; phone: 813-968-8863; email: Tom@FocusedBaseball.com.

CHAPTER 17

How To Market Yourself

Michael Bono
Coach/Marketing Specialist

Previous chapters have focused on building your knowledge and skills to make you a marketable player. In the world of baseball you must know everything about your ability as well as everything about your competition. The key to every successful marketing campaign is the development of a business plan. Once the plan is developed it must be executed. Then you need to reassess it annually to see if it is moving you toward your desired results. My goal is to help you develop a plan by:

- Understanding the time to market by developing an action based timeline.
- Identifying the market size by understanding the odds and chances of succeeding.
- Determining what your skills and ability are worth and the types of scholarships that are being awarded.
- Identifying your target market by choosing the right school.
- Developing some high-yield tactics to successfully execute the plan in order to get noticed.

High School Planning - Timeline

Freshman Year – Start developing good classroom and home study habits. Learn to manage your time. This will become more important every year. Academics play a significant role in college baseball. Some high schools have freshman teams while others only have junior varsity and varsity. If you fail to make the JV team as a freshman, don't give up. Play spring ball in a community league. Work harder and get stronger.

Sophomore Year – Continue to hit the books hard. Meet with your guidance counselor and tell him/her of your desire to play college baseball. Now is the time to adjust your academic core courses to meet NCAA and college requirements. Following your high school season play as many summer baseball games as possible. Playing against the strongest competition available will improve your game and better prepare you for varsity competition. Watch your local newspaper for pro try-out camps. These will get you some free exposure and prepare you for future showcases.

Junior Year – Starting with the fall do not let up on academics. In September send out your first contact letters to selected colleges. (Letter types and formats will be discussed later in this chapter). Register with the NCAA Initial Eligibility Clearinghouse (your guidance counselor should have these forms). Register for fall ACT and SAT standardized tests to avoid conflicts with your spring high school schedule. Most students take these tests at least twice. In the case of the SAT you can combine the highest verbal and math scores from multiple tests. Check out the *NCAA.org* to familiarize yourself with NCAA admissions/eligibility requirements.

Spring - Send out your spring high school schedules. Prepare a videotape to be sent out when requested (do not send unsolicited tapes). Plan school visits to as many schools as possible this spring and summer. Don't be shy; write a letter to the coach asking if the school has Junior Days. All of these are unofficial visits, which means that the college cannot pay for any part of the visit.

<u>Summer</u> - Focus this summer on attending one or two select or advanced college camps. This will help you compare your abilities against some of the best players. The college coaches will be able to do the same. July 1st is the first day that phone contact from a college coach is allowed. July can be a *make or break* month for you. Excellent performances in a couple of showcases that are well attended by college coaches and pro scouts can open a lot of doors for you. Likewise a poor performance can cause a recruiting setback. Continue to look for and attend free pro try-out camps. Most of the pro scouts have good relationships with the local college coaches. Even if you do not feel that you are a pro prospect, ask the scout if you can use his name on a college questionnaire. Be sure you get his name correct for any correspondence.

Senior Year – One final reminder that academics will play a significant role in where and if you get a chance to play college baseball. Personally I feel your senior year is the best and most critical time for exposure to college coaches and pro scouts. If you live in an area where fall baseball is played and you have an opportunity to play on a scout or showcase travel team, you should make every effort to join such a club. Many colleges take advantage of the early signing period (usually a seven day period in mid-November) and this fall season gives them an excellent time to see prospective players during their off-season. The fall also kicks off the new pro scouting year. Most scouts take a couple months off after the June draft and start up again in October in regions that play fall baseball. Update college coaches with your fall schedule. Remember you can contact college coaches anytime, however, only after July 1st following your junior year can they call you.

<u>Spring</u> - If you are fortunate enough to sign during the fall early signing period, congratulations are in order. Continue to work hard and have a great senior season. If you don't sign early and are offered an official visit, prepare yourself with a list of questions. Be prepared for any question the college may ask of you. Don't waste your time with a visit if you have no intention of attending the school. Your senior season is upon you. Work hard, play hard and have fun.

Understanding The Odds

The following are documented facts published in 2001 regarding the probability of your playing collegiate baseball or playing baseball professionally.

- Less than 6 percent of high school senior baseball players will go on to play baseball at an NCAA member institution.
- Less than 11 percent of NCAA senior baseball players will get drafted by a Major League Baseball (MLB) team.

STUDENT ATHLETES	BASEBALL
High School Athletes	455,300
High School Senior Athletes	130,100
NCAA Student-Athletes	25,700
NCAA Freshman Roster Positions	7,300
NCAA Senior Student Athletes	5,700
NCAA Student Athletes Drafted	600
% High School to NCAA	5.6
% NCAA to Professional	10.5
% High School to Professional	0.5

Scholarships

In Division I or Division II baseball, don't expect a full athletic scholarship. It just does not happen. Can a baseball player potentially attend college and have his tuition, books, room and board all paid however? Yes. This is where your four years of academic work pay off. Keep in mind that fully funded Division I schools only have 11.7 scholarships, and Division II schools only have 9. Many well-known Division II baseball programs have less than the maximum allowable scholarships. Both of these divisions are allowed to divide these scholarships up in many ways. Some schools talk in terms of dollars while others make offers in terms of percentages or a combination of the two. Here is an example: 25% of tuition, 100% of books and $1,500 toward room and board. This should be considered a very good baseball offer at a Division I school.

Academics scholarships are normally dollar grants to be applied initially toward tuition and books, but can then be used for room and board if funds remain. Some states, such as Florida, offer in-state Bright Futures academic tuition awards of 75% and 100% of the cost of public universities for students and athletes who attain a 3.0 GPA during the high school career and score at least 970 on the SAT or 20 on the ACT.

At the Junior College level as many as 24 full scholarships are offered. In some states these can be broken down like Division I and Division II while in other states they must be offered as full packages.

Division III schools do not offer athletic scholarships and receive very little media coverage but offer a lot of tradition and history. As you can see from the table below, more young athletes play baseball at Division III than any NCAA division. As far as education is concerned these schools are among the finest in the country. Fully funded NAIA schools can offer 12 scholarships. These schools combine a very competitive level of baseball with a personalized and informal educational environment.

Finding The Right College Program

Here is a breakdown by division of schools that offer collegiate baseball programs.

DIVISION	TEAMS	PARTICIPANTS
NCAA D I	282	9,391
NCAA D II	224	6,922
NCAA D III	332	9,230
NAIA	332	9,960
NJCAA D I	182	5,460
NJCAA D II	128	3,840
NJCAA D III	83	2,490

Most likely the coach at the college where you will someday play doesn't even know you play baseball. You and your parents need to take an aggressive approach to college selection and recruiting to avoid financial hardship and heartbreak. Your high school coach can help, but you have to take the initiative and direct the coach as to what you are interested in and how you need his help. Make sure that he is willing to support your effort before you include his name on a questionnaire. Don't be afraid to use your American Legion or scout team coach as a reference. A lot of these coaches have more contacts than high school coaches.

Choose a school where you feel you can get playing time. Studying the rosters of the schools that you are interested in attending is very important. If you're a catcher, don't choose a school that has five underclassmen catchers. If you are a pitcher, look for schools that have a predominantly junior and senior pitching staff. Choose a school environment where you would be happy should your athletic career come to an abrupt end. Choose a place where you can complete your education and earn a degree.

How To Get Noticed

Most players choose a combination of direct mailing to college coaches as well as attending college camps and showcases. Here are some very critical *Do*s and *Do Not*s as you begin contacting selected schools and coaches.

- **Do** address a college coach with his last name in the salutation. For example, *Dear Coach Frady*. 95% of all letters that start with *Dear Coach* are tossed in the trash. College coaches are not impressed that you didn't take the time to even find out their names.

- **Do** complete and return all questionnaires that you receive. If you have no interest in the school, include in your response that you are flattered by their interest but at this time you are currently pursuing other opportunities. Coaches have a relatively large network and they frequently forward questionnaires between schools.

- ◆ **Do** call the baseball office to confirm the receipt of your letter or questionnaire. Leave a message if the coach is not available. This phone contact will give the coach an idea of how well you communicate and a basis to start formulating an impression of you.
- ◆ **Do not** call the coach at his home unless he specifically requests that you call him there.
- ◆ **Do not** write a novel. Keep correspondence to one page if possible.
- ◆ **Do not** stretch the truth about academic or athletic abilities. There is no quicker way to lose credibility with a coach than to misstate the facts.

Statistics, media articles, and high school coach references are all important, but even combined they do not compare to the college coach's personal evaluation of you as a player and a person.

As with most things in life first impressions are very important. Letters should be typed, unless your handwriting is exceptionally neat and legible. Keep your initial contact letter brief. Identify yourself, your school and graduating class. Express interest in attending the school and your desire to learn more about the school and its baseball program. Attach a brief information sheet outlining both your athletic and academic accomplishments.

Be aware that NCAA rules do not allow direct personal contact or phone contact with a high school baseball player until July 1, after your junior year. However, written correspondence is allowed at anytime.

It is important that college coaches have your spring, summer and fall schedules in order for them to watch you play in live-game situations. Many coaches will not offer scholarship money to a player they have not seen play in a game. Many scholarships are offered during the fall early signing period

Videotapes should not be sent unsolicited. The development of a videotape is a good idea, but it should be no longer than four to five minutes. An accompanying correspondence should describe the contents of the tape. The tapes for position players should include fielding and throwing from position and the hitting segments should show multiple angles. Pitchers should throw from both the wind-up and set positions. Twelve to sixteen pitches are all that is needed depending on number of kinds of pitches that you throw.

If you don't hear from some schools, you'll need to follow up with another letter. Be persistent. Sometimes you might not hear from a school because they may be loaded at your particular position.

I recently had a player who transferred from New England with good SAT scores, a high GPA, excellent 60-yard dash time, and a throwing velocity in the mid to high 80s and still he didn't receive a response from some colleges. The player's package included certain items that aren't available to most players – an article about him in *Collegiate Baseball Magazine*, and a letter of recommendation from one of the best known college coaches in the country. This experience pointed out to me the importance of the college coach's personal evaluation of the player. After this experience the player participated in a very strong fall scout program and then took the next step in how to get noticed: During Christmas vacation he attended a baseball camp at the college he most wanted to attend. There he caught the eye of the school's head recruiter. This resulted in a verbal commitment by the coaching staff that led to the signing of a national letter of intent following a successful senior season.

Most of the coaches from strong baseball programs attend the big name showcases such as Team ONE and Perfect Game. Coaches and scouts have limited time available to them and while ideally they would like to see each player in four or five games to get a feel for the player's ability, it usually doesn't work that way. In certain cases they depend on the opinion of other trusted coaches but usually they like to see you perform for themselves.

My players have had the most success in attending a school camp, clinic league, or a camp where they knew their selected school's coach was working. Here the coach sees you over an extended period of time. He sees you with several at-bats. He notices your work ethic and other skills. He develops a feel for you as a person. If you attend the camp multiple times during your high school career, he can also observe your physical development.

Following a college camp ask the coach for his honest opinion of your abilities and whether you might fit into their program. If you are interested in a Division I school and he feels you are a Division II or NAIA player, he will tell you. Once again this is one coach's opinion. Coaches aren't always right, but they usually are pretty good at knowing who can play for them. Recruiting isn't an exact science. No coach is infallible and they all make mistakes, but typically they are pretty honest when it comes to assessing ability and whether or not that ability will fit into their program

There are many showcases to choose from. I have listed a few of the better known ones. The following *invitation only* showcases usually require the recommendation of a college coach or professional scout. This tends to keep the talent at a pretty high level and encourages coaches to attend.

Area Code Games	*www.areacodebaseball.org*
Perfect Game	*www.perfectgame.org*
Team One	*www.teamonebaseball.com*
College Select	*www.collegeselect.org*
Top 96 Showcase	*www.top96.com*

The following are open showcases that run multiple times during the year throughout the country and anyone can attend.

All American Talent	*www.thehitdoctor.com*
Baseball Factory	*www.baseballfactory.com*
Blue Grey Classic	*www.impactprospects.com*

These are just of few of the better-known showcases. There are dozens of additional showcases around the country. One thing that a good showcase can tell a player is where he might stand compared with other players. In previous chapters we have already seen what scouts and coaches look for. If a player can throw a baseball at 90 MPH and run the 60 in 6.6, he knows he is probably going to get some looks from Division I schools. The key point here is that you may have the best tools in the world, but if no one knows about them, you won't get noticed. You need to be seen and sometimes a good showcase can get you that attention.

If you can't afford to attend multiple showcases, perhaps you can attend one key event. If you don't have the money, write or e-mail the showcase and let them know of your financial situation. If you can get the recommendation of your high school or summer coach and possibly a regional scout, they sometimes can get your registration fee reduced or waived.

All Coaches and Recruiters Are Not Created Equal

Most of the college coaches who I have met are honest men, and as they recruit players they are looking for true student-athletes. However, some only care about you as a player, not a person. Watch out for the coach who talks more about putting down the competition than he does about building up his own team. On the other hand watch out for a coach who only talks about his program and his personal accomplishments and goals. Look for a coach who cares about you as a person. A coach who takes the time to listen to your expectations and shares his with you has both parties' best interests at heart. If he doesn't seem to care or show interest in you other than just baseball, then it may not be the right program for you. Watch out for the coach who promises you a starting position. Freshmen do start but they are the exception and not the norm. The honest recruiter will tell you what his expectations are for incoming freshmen. Watch out for a coach who offers a four-year scholarship. NCAA allows only a one-year, renewable scholarship. Watch out for a coach who puts you in touch with a booster from the college. NCAA permits no contact with boosters. Watch out for the coach who promises you easy professors or an easy schedule. He has no interest in you other than baseball. Look for the coach who shares with you all the pluses and minuses of attending his school. The best coaches in the top programs realize that college is more than just baseball. It's also academic work, campus life, and you as a person.

Mike Bono

Sports Information
Director/Webmaster
Coach/Marketing Specialist

Mike Bono has coached amateur baseball for the past twenty-one years. He played Division I baseball at Murray State University from 1969 to 1973. His teams have won Florida championships in Pony, Babe Ruth, American Legion and AAU baseball. As a charter member of the AAU Baseball Committee he worked closely with Chet Lemon to grow Florida into one of the nation's largest programs. For the past two years Mike has served as Sports Information Director and Webmaster for Lake Mary High School's nationally ranked baseball program providing weekly articles to *Baseball America, Collegiate Baseball, ESPN* and *USA Today.* In 2000, the Central Florida Suns (17 & Under) competed for AAU's national championship, finishing third in the nation. In 2001, he sponsored and coached American Legion Post 53 that compiled a 51-2 record. He also managed the Seminole Scout team that finished third in the 2001 Perfect Game 64-team Wood Bat National Championship.

Mike is a founding partner of the Executive Sports Club of Orlando and also represents *Computer Associates International, Inc.* (CA), a four-billion-dollar software company. He joined CA in 1986 and has served as Sales Executive, National Account Manager and Divisional Vice President. In 2001, Mike was recognized as CA's North American sales leader. CA develops software that manages e-Business. Product brands include Unicenter, BrightStor and eTrust.

Mike and his wife, Sheila, have four children, Mickey, Kim and twin sons, Ryan and Kyle, who are attending the University of Central Florida on baseball scholarships.

You can reach Mike at Michael.Bono@ca.com or 407-687-6600.

CHAPTER 18

Mini-Mites

Section A: Why You Should Practice With Wood Bats

Almost every great hitting instructor tells his students to practice with wood. This is good advice for every high school and college ballplayer. Practice with wood and use metal in games. Why practice with wood? Most ballplayers would rather hit with metal for two reasons:
1) The sweet spot is bigger, giving them a larger surface area to drive the ball, and
2) The ball goes farther. While the latest metal bats are supposed to be the equivalent of wood, metal bats on average drive the ball anywhere from 10-20% farther than wood bats do.

Here's why.
1) A wood bat is heavier than a metal bat and it takes more strength to get the bat through the hitting zone. In other words it takes a real man to swing a wood bat.

2) A wood bat is harder to control. There is more chance of error

and less room for mistakes. The swing has to be true to be successful with wood.

3) The sweet-spot is much smaller with a wood bat. You can't hit a ball with a wood bat on the trademark and expect it to go far. With a metal bat a hitter can believe he is a much better hitter than he is. It takes real skill to hit a ball with the smaller sweet-spot of a wood bat.

4) Balls come off a wood bat at 10-15 MPH slower than off a metal bat. Fewer balls get through the defense. It takes great skill to hit with wood.

5) Because of the heavier weight, a hitter has to be much quicker with his swing than with a metal bat.

6) The swing speed will be decreased as will the exit speed of the ball.

Finally wood bats should be used in high school and college scrimmages as a safety factor to protect both pitchers and infielders. If you are not using a wood bat, begin using one now. It will make you a better hitter in the long run.

Dave Hudgens, Assistant Player Development Director of the Oakland As says that a majority of the young players he sees coming out of high school and college do not know how to use a wood bat. The ball may not go as far in practice, but using a wood bat will make you a better hitter, and that's what it's all about.

If you don't like the feel of wood, perhaps you could get started with a metal/wood bat. These bats have the metal handle that you are used to, but the wood barrel that you need to become a better hitter. You can check the bats out at *www.metalwoodbats.com.*

Also, Hoosier Bat Company makes a nice wood bat. Their three-piece *Woodforce Bats* cost $45.00 each. You can ship three bats for $5.00. Their solid *Ash Bats* are $30.00 each. Visit Hoosier's site at *www.HoosierBat.com* or call them at 1-800-228-3787.

Section B: What The American Cancer Society Says About Smokeless Tobacco

Many high school and college baseball players have gotten into the bad habit of using smokeless tobacco or dip. From 1976 to 1994 American adults smoking cigarettes declined from 36% to 26%. However, during this same time, there was a resurgence in the use of all forms of smokeless tobacco – plug, leaf, and snuff. The greatest cause for concern is the sharply increased use of *dipping* snuff.

Smokeless tobacco use is promoted as a safe alternative to cigarette smoking and is advertised as a masculine, attractive, and socially acceptable practice. In reality, smokeless tobacco increases the risk of oral cancer and other health practices. Here are the facts that every ballplayer should consider:

- Tobacco use is a known cause of cancer. Smokeless tobacco is *not* a safe substitute for cigarettes.

- Approximately 4,000,000 adults are current users of smokeless tobacco. Use is increasing, especially among young males.

- 20% of male high school students use smokeless tobacco.

- Unburned tobacco contains the carcinogenic nitrosamines NNN and NNK, which have tumor-initiating properties.

- The Third National Cancer Survey found that men who used smokeless tobacco incurred nearly a four-fold increased risk of oral cancer. Long-term users had a fifty-fold increase risk of cancer of the gums.

- Gingival recession is a common result of smokeless tobacco use.

- Heavy metals such as lead and cadmium have been found in smokeless tobacco.

- Studies show users of smokeless tobacco had elevated blood levels of nicotine similar to those produced by cigarettes. Smokeless tobacco users experience changes in heart rate and blood pressure.

- Benign oral lesions may occur after only a few years of use of smokeless tobacco.

- Smokeless tobacco is extremely addictive and makes the user nicotine dependent.

- Leukoplakia is a condition characterized by white, wrinkled, thickened patches in the places of the mouth where tobacco is held. Most chronic (habitual, long-time) users will develop Leukoplakia. Leukoplakia cases often become cancer cases.

It's a proven fact: Dipping causes lip, cheek, tongue and other types of oral cancer, and the longer you dip, the greater your chances of getting oral cancer. A dipper's gums start receding, and the dip damages mouth tissue beyond repair. When he was 12 years old, Sean Marsee began dipping. He thought it was safe. Six years later he had cancer in the very spot where he once put dip. At 19 Sean Marsee was dead.

Dipping is addictive, period. The nicotine in dip is a drug. Don't get hooked.

If you are currently using the product, stop now before it causes you major problems later. The NCAA has banned all forms of smokeless tobacco. Proper medical help can show you ways of kicking the habit. Sugarless gum is a lot safer alternative.

For more information, call the American Cancer Society toll free at 1-800-ACS-2345 or visit their Internet site at *www.cancer.org*.

Section C: Why Good Grades Are Important

Getting good grades in high school is important for a number of reasons. First, you need minimum grades or you probably won't qualify to play baseball at a Division I, Division II or Division III institution. For instance, the minimum requirement to play at a Division II college is a 2.0 GPA (C Average) and combined 820 on your SATs. The requirements are even higher for a Division I institution. The lower your GPA, the higher SAT you need to get. Under the new proposed Division I requirements you could technically receive the lowest SAT score possible (400) and still qualify to play college ball if your GPA is high enough

Minimums to play are one thing, but another key point to remember is baseball scholarship money is difficult to get. The average Division I program carries between 32 to 35 players with only 11.7 scholarships available. It's obvious that not every player can get a full baseball scholarship. In most cases, players only get a partial scholarship, and most money is allocated to high profile positions like pitchers, key infielders and power hitters.

Academic scholarships are very important to ballplayers, and they aren't based on financial need. They are based on merit. If you get good grades throughout high school and good SAT or ACT scores, you have an excellent chance of receiving an academic scholarship. Each school is, of course, unique in their requirements for academic money, but you can usually expect the cut-off to be around a 3.0 GPA and 1100 SAT. Some schools may have a 3.5 GPA and 1100 SAT requirement. Good grades and good scores like these could be worth several thousand dollars a year to you.

Maybe you have a decent GPA, but didn't do well on your SAT exam. If you have trouble with this type of test, you may need to take a computer course or a class on improving your SAT test scores. Classes can get expensive and run several hundred dollars. Computer courses can run from fifty to a couple hundred dollars and usually give you several practice exams and tips for taking the test and answering the questions. If you apply yourself, you could get an increase of 50-100 points. This could be enough to get you a scholarship. One company we mention on the Peak Power Baseball website is www.kaplan.com. Kaplan is a leader in this industry, and they have several alternative programs to choose from.

Also remember that baseball doesn't last forever. A good education is very important to you down the road. I have seen students sign professional contracts and for one reason or another, they no longer play baseball. Their good habits in high school and college, however, translated into making them well conversed in a number of subjects, with skills they can use in any profession or career.

Play hard and study hard and it will all pay off for you in the end.

CHAPTER 19

David Eckstein's Dream

Rod Fergerson
Coach, Sanford, Florida

When a reporter asked why he played so hard, Joe DiMaggio responded by saying, "Because there might be someone (at the game) who never saw me play before."

When a reporter asked the same question of the Anaheim Angels' David Eckstein, his answer was, "Because I don't know how to play any other way." This is the way David Eckstein plays. As he puts it, "Since I was little, I was always told to play hard. No matter how good or bad you are, you can always play hard. As a player, the only thing you can control in the game is how hard you play. I don't have the greatest ability in the world, and I wouldn't be here on talent alone. If I let up, someone will take my job."

When I first met David Eckstein, the first thing I noticed about him was his intensity. He had a gleam of determination in his eyes. When he showed up at practice he certainly wasn't imposing player physically. He was just a little guy who said he wanted to be a major leaguer someday. This dream of his came from a kid who lacked size, who didn't have the greatest arm, and who wasn't the greatest hitter. But these words came from someone who impressed me right from the beginning. There was something about this young man's confidence that really struck me, and I wasn't going to be the one to say his dream was probably just that - a dream.

David didn't start for his high school team as a freshman, but he got the opportunity when he was a sophomore. David played second base and my son, Scott, played shortstop. I think second base is probably David's most natural position, but his success at shortstop with the Angels doesn't surprise me at all. In fact, David would be successful behind the plate if you asked him to play there.

David was a good ballplayer throughout high school, but certainly not a superstar. He was an All-State performer for two years, and he played on a State championship team. At the end of his high school career, however, he didn't receive a single scholarship offer. Every coach I'd talk to would tell me that David was too small for the rigors of college ball. David was certainly discouraged by the lack of interest from college coaches, but he didn't give up. He decided he wanted to go to the University of Florida where some of his brothers and sisters had gone and was going to be a walk-on and try and make the team. The chances of any walk-on making a top Division I team are slim, and with David's size, he really was at a disadvantage.

David did make the team, however, and when a teammate ahead of him decided to transfer to another school, a door opened for him in his sophomore year. He jumped at the opportunity. David ended up All-Southeastern Conference twice and an All-American his senior year in 1996. When David graduated from Florida, he held several Florida offensive records.

Many people say David has been lucky to get where he is today. I believe it does take a little luck to get to the majors, but I also know that David has always made it a habit of being in the right place at the right time and making the most of his opportunities. Sometimes it just takes one person who believes in you to get you going. I believed in David, his college coach believed in him, and a former major league scout for the Red Sox, Luke Wrenn, believed enough in him to give him a contract. David ended up being drafted by the Boston Red Sox in the 19th round in 1997.

David posted averages over .300 for the Sox at three levels before he was sent to Triple A Pawtucket in the year 2000. Unfortunately, or fortunately (depending on the way you look at it), David only hit .246 at Pawtucket and was taken off the 40-man roster when the Angels picked him up off waiver. While there didn't seem to be a place for David at Anaheim, he got another break when Adam Kennedy broke his finger during spring training in 2001. David filled in at second and really impressed manager Mike Scioscia with his hustle and hard play, and he ended up starting for the Angels on opening day.

With David hitting over .300 in April, Scioscia had a tough decision to make when Kennedy came off the disabled list. Scioscia decided to shift David to shortstop, and that's where he's been ever since. He ended up with a .355 on-base percentage as a rookie for the Angels and has become an ideal lead-off hitter. David continues to do what he has always done - work hard, play smart and hustle. He has a good eye for the strike zone, takes a lot of pitches, and irritates pitchers by fouling off numerous pitches. He also led the majors in getting hit by a pitch. He sprays the ball all over the field, is a great bunter, and does whatever he can to get on base. He's a good base stealer, and fast enough and smart enough to take the extra base at every opportunity.

As far as his defense is concerned, it's as one scout pointed out during the World Series, "Just enough". He does "just enough" to get you out. He makes up for his lack of height with excellent range and an accurate, although not overpowering, arm

What Peak Power Baseball is all about is making the most of what you have - your God-given talents. It's about maximizing your physical tools and being mentally prepared to play the game. I see no greater example of this than David Eckstein.

One reason coaches have always liked David is because of his work ethic. The way he goes about playing the game is very infectious. He will embarrass the rest of the team with his work ethic, and as a coach, you have to appreciate an intangible quality like that. David always gives 100%. He never was the biggest, the fastest or the best hitter. He is, however, an example of how hard work and intensity can take you a lot further than mere physical attributes.

David never jogged when he could sprint. He never left the field early if someone was there to hit him extra ground balls. He was a good listener who was willing to try new things. If it worked for him, he would stick with it. If it didn't, he wouldn't. The only negative you could find is that he didn't have a lot of size. However, for a kid his size he is very strong. He makes me think of an old Spencer Tracy - Katherine Hepburn movie where Tracy says of his athlete superstar, Hepburn, "There's not much meat on her, but what's there is choice." And with David, it's choice and natural. David is a perfect example of someone who has made it without the artificial assistance of steroids.

David was a good kid from a good family. He went to church every Sunday, he didn't swear, he was not a big spender, and he never got down on himself. He had pretty good speed and a pretty good arm, but his biggest asset was his tremendous drive and work ethic. It's something he would have applied to any field he entered. He just hoped to be lucky enough to have it be baseball. Keep in mind, however, that everyone, or most everyone, who makes it to the majors is a hard worker. Probably 2-3% make it on talent alone. David is someone who made it happen without overpowering physical tools. Now, with the 2002 season complete, all of David's hard work has paid off. He now has what every young ballplayer dreams of - a World Series Ring. He's also probably going to receive a nice new contract. Sometime good guys do win, and David is a perfect example of it!

I enjoyed coaching David and watching his career develop over the years. Even when the Red Sox gave up on him, David didn't give up on himself. I think the whole point behind Peak Power Baseball is that a player needs to take what God has given him and make the most of it. David Eckstein is a perfect example of what can happen when this is done.

Rod Fergerson

Coach, Sanford, Florida

Coach Rod Ferguson started his baseball career in 1958 as a bat-boy for the Detroit Tigers. After an injury ended his college-playing career, he decided to enter coaching. After 32 years as an active coach, Rod's teams have attained over 2,500 victories in high school, American Legion and Scout team baseball, making Rod one of the most successful coaches in the country with the most wins. His American Legion Team Post 53 in Sanford, Florida, has been in eight of the last nine State finals, has won four of the last six State titles and won the American Legion World Series in 1997.

In 2002, he was named the Diamond Club of Florida Amateur Coach of the Year.

Rod can be reached at rferguson@cfl.rr.com.

CHAPTER 20

Calling On A Higher Power

Jim Vigue

When I was a senior in high school, I was a pretty fair football player. In a game against the Harvard freshman team, I didn't do too well and found myself on the bench during the next game. I got in for a few plays after that and did all right, but I wasn't convinced I'd be in the starting backfield in our season's final game. I felt really alone and disappointed and began to doubt my abilities.

I had a talk with the assistant coach and told him I was losing confidence and didn't really know how to snap myself out of it. I couldn't admit my doubts to my teammates or my coach, and I really didn't know where to turn. My assistant coach gave me a copy of *The Power of Positive Thinking,* by Dr. Norman Vincent Peale. From the first chapter I was hooked, and I felt a surge of inner power and renewed confidence. By Monday's practice I felt I could do anything. I had a great week of practice and by game time on Saturday, I was again in the starting backfield. The first time I touched the ball I scored an 80-yard touchdown. Before the afternoon was over, I had touched the ball five times and had scored four touchdowns – one on a run from scrimmage, another via a kickoff return, another on a punt return, and the final one on an 85-yard pass play. I had scored about every way possible, and all of the touchdowns were from over 75 yards out. Well, this sold me on *The Power of Positive Thinking* to say the least.

When my son was in junior high school, he was the only seventh grader on an eighth-grade baseball team, and he didn't think he would get a chance to play much. Even though he thought he should be a starter, he didn't play at all in the first game of the season. He came home discouraged, but I told him to stay positive and that he had to be ready when he got his chance to play. I gave him a couple of chapters to read from *The Power of Positive Thinking*, and told him to believe in himself. At the next game, the player who was supposed to pitch didn't show up for the game, and the coach asked if anyone else had pitched before. My son and one other player put their hands up. The coach thought about it for a minute, then said, "Okay, Kris, you pitch today, and we'll see how you do." To make a long story short, my son pitched a no-hitter that afternoon, and if that wasn't enough, he hit a grand slam and two three-run triples for a total of 10 RBIs. The sad thing was, I showed up late for the game because I didn't think he was going to start, and I missed the grand slam. Kris went on to be a four-year starter in high school, and as this is being written, he is playing for a nationally ranked Division I university. He's definitely someone who believes in the *Power of Positive Thinking*.

As a result of this experience, I continue to hand out Peale's book to young athletes. The book has sold over 20,000,000 copies and has influenced the lives of millions.

In life as well as in sports, it is tough to be alone. There may be times when you feel like the whole world is against you, and you doubt that you have the ability to go forward. Sometimes you will need someone on your side who will always be there and who never waivers. There is a proverb in Ecclesiastes that says, *Two can accomplish more than twice as much as one, for the results can be much better. If one falls the other pulls him up, but if a man falls when he is alone, he's in trouble.* (Ecclesiates 4:9 TLB)

I guess the key is that none of us wants to be alone. We want to believe that someone is always with us. In my case it was Christ, but the simple fact of believing that someone is always with us by our side is very powerful.

As athletes we often feel inadequate and doubt ourselves. Peale's book offers a number of very simple, workable rules for learning to believe in ourselves and practice our faith. Taking these rules to heart can ultimately make a major difference in how we see ourselves, and how we develop as athletes.

Let's go over each of Peale's rules and adapt them to baseball:

1. Formulate and stamp indelibly on your mind a mental picture of yourselves as succeeding. Hold this picture tenaciously. Never permit it to fade. Your mind will seek to develop this picture. Never think of yourself as failing; never doubt the reality of the mental image. That is most dangerous, for the mind always tries to complete what it pictures. So always picture "success" no matter how badly things seem to be going at the moment. [1]

A lot of athletes have the physical attributes to make it to the top levels in baseball. There are a lot of 6.6 sprinters who have 90-MPH arm velocity and a good bat, but they don't make it. There are numerous reasons why this happens, but quite often it is because they can't handle the mental pressures of the game. They get in a little slump and begin to doubt their abilities. They picture themselves failing instead of succeeding. It is absolutely paramount that you picture yourself succeeding as a ballplayer. Failure from lack of ability is one thing, but to fail because of mental self-doubt is unacceptable. Never permit failure to enter your mind, and your chances of success multiply tremendously.

2. Whenever a negative thought concerning your personal power comes to mind, deliberately voice a positive thought to cancel it out. [2]

---

[1] Reprinted with the permission of Simon & Schuster, Inc., from THE POWER OF POSITIVE THINKING by Norman Vincent Peale. Copyright @ 1952, 1956 by Prentice-Hall, Inc.; copyright renewed @ 1980, 1984 by Norman Vincent Peale.

Positive self-talk is vitally important to a ballplayer. When you go to the plate your attitude can't be, *I can't hit this guy.* You have to go to the plate totally confident that no pitcher will be able to beat you. If you are on the mound facing a tough hitter, your attitude has to be, *He will not beat me. He will not hit my best pitch.* In sports there always has to be a winner and a loser, but positive self-talk puts the odds in your favor.

3. Do not build obstacles in your imagination. Depreciate every so-called obstacle. Minimize them. Difficulties must be studied and efficiently dealt with to be eliminated, but they must be seen for only what they are. They must not be inflated by fear thoughts. [3]

My son Kris was told over and over that his size (5'9" – 165 pounds) would prevent him from playing at a top Division I program. He had it in his mind that this one liability would prevail over all of his assets (bat speed, foot speed, arm velocity) and it would prevent him from reaching his goal.

Yes, some coaches believe bigger players are more durable, but not everyone in the majors is 6'2" – 195 pounds. I urged my son to emphasize his strong points and not concentrate on his size. I told him to look for coaches and programs where size didn't matter. He eventually found a program where two players under 5'9" had signed major league contracts the year before. He found a program where performance, not size, mattered. He ended up signing a national letter of intent with a top 25 program in Division I. His goal was realized, but only after he minimized his size and maximized his abilities. Don't hold yourself back by building up obstacles in your head that aren't really obstacles but only minor problems that need to be overcome.

4. Do not be awestruck by other people and try to copy them. Nobody can be you as efficiently as YOU can. Remember also that most people, despite their confident appearance and demeanor, are often as scared as you are and as doubtful of themselves. [4]

Keep in mind that in baseball there is no one right way to do things. All great hitters don't have the same swing. Don't try to be someone you aren't. A great hitting instructor once told me that he never tries to change a good hitter's swing. He may tinker with it, he may refine it a bit, but he never changes it. If someone has made it to the higher levels of baseball, he probably already has a pretty good swing. If you're 5'9" and 160 pounds, you probably won't have a swing like Sammy Sosa or Barry Bonds. Be yourself. Emphasize and build upon your unique characteristics as a ballplayer. Don't try to be someone you aren't.

5. Ten times a day repeat these dynamic words, "If God be for us, who can be against us? (Romans 8:31) 5

There will be days when it seems everyone is against you – your coach, your teammates, the fans, and the press. These are the times when you need a higher power – someone to fall back on, someone who will be there in-spite of the fact that you went 0 for 5. It is very reassuring to know that whatever is happening in your life there is someone who will stand by you. When you get into that batter's box or step on the mound, remember someone magnificent is by your side.

6. Get a competent counselor to help you understand why you do what you do. Learn the origin of your inferiority and self-doubt feelings, which often begin in childhood. Self-knowledge leads to a cure. 6

Many good ballplayers will never make it all the way because they never believe they can. The mental side of the game is often overlooked. This is why we included chapters in this book on the mental aspects of baseball. If you really doubt your natural ability, you need to speak with a professional experienced in this area who will hopefully help you. Getting to the root of this problem could make the difference in whether you succeed or fail. Don't let something in your past hold you back. If you doubt yourself, you need to find out why and do something about it.

7. Ten times each day practice the following affirmation, repeating it out loud if possible, "I can do all things through Christ which strengtheneth me." (Philippians 4:13) Repeat those words NOW. That major statement is the most powerful antidote on earth to inferiority thoughts. [7]

A ballplayer needs to believe that he will be successful. Self-doubt is a killer. This statement reminds me of the Little Engine That Could that kept repeating, *I think I can. I think I can. I think I can.* When you step into that batter's box, you need to believe that you can *do all things*. You need to believe that you will be successful. Statistics tell us that hitting is an act of failure. Even great hitters fail six times out of ten. You can improve your odds by believing that you will be successful and that God is strengthening you. *Outer Power* is generated by your arms and legs. *Inner Power* is generated by confidence and the belief that a higher power is strengthening you and working through you.

8. Make a true estimate of your own ability, then raise it ten percent. Do not become egotistical, but develop a wholesome self-respect. Believe in your own God-released powers. [8]

As you hopefully learned from the chapter, *The Magic 5%*, ballplayers more often underestimate their abilities than overestimate them. It is easy to lose confidence in your abilities. It is easy to believe that you don't have what it takes. It is like the ballplayer who has a chance to sign with a Division I college, but ends up attending a Division III school. There are no guarantees in life, but with all things being equal, you shouldn't settle for anything less than the best – nothing ventured, nothing gained! Why not test yourself with the best? Perhaps by raising in your own mind an estimate of your abilities you can mentally take the plunge. It is smart to remember that you can always go down, but sometimes it's impossible to go up. If in your mind's eye you visualize that you are better than you are, perhaps you will eventually get to that higher level.

9. Put yourself in God's hands. To do that simply state, "I am in God's hands." Then believe you are NOW receiving all the power you need. "Feel" it flowing into you. Affirm that "the kingdom of God is within you" (Luke 17:21) in the form of adequate power to meet life's demands. 9

Believing that you have the power inside you and that God's presence is indeed part of you gives you a tremendous boost of energy and confidence. It can get awfully lonely at the plate, but it doesn't have to be you alone against the world. Try this technique and see if it works for you as it has worked for so many athletes.

10. Remind yourself that God is with you and nothing can defeat you. Believe that you now RECEIVE power from Him. 10

We've discussed how an extra 5% in physical power can catapult you from an average performer or prospect to someone who is really noticed. The same can happen with an extra 5% of mental power. Often a slight mental edge is all you need. Having a greater power on your side could give you the mental edge you need to overcome the inevitable negative thoughts that can hold you back from great success.

These are just ideas from *one* chapter of *The Power of Positive Thinking*. The book is loaded with ideas and suggestions that will help you be a better person and a better baseball player.

If you would like to receive a free condensed edition of *The Power of Positive Thinking,* simply write to:

The Power of Positive Thinking
66 East Main Street
Pawling, NY 12564

Or E-mail them at: *blessings@guideposts.org*

1,2,3,4,5,6,7,8,9,10 – Reprinted with the permission of Simon & Schuster, Inc., from THE POWER OF POSITIVE THINKING by Norman Vincent Peale. Copyright @ 1952, 1956 by Prentice-Hall, Inc.; copyright renewed @ 1980, 1984 by Norman Vincent Peale. Acknowledgement is made to the Peale Foundation, Inc. for permission to reprint excerpts from *The Power of Positive Thinking* by Norman Vincent Peale.

The Final Pitch

By Jim Vigue

If you've read this entire book, you have proven that you are sincerely interested in maximizing your performance and bringing your game to the next level.

If you have a dream of playing college or professional baseball, success can be yours. All the strategies you need are now in your hands. You know what you need to do to get to the top.

- You need to focus on proper nutrition and be aware of what you put into your body.

- You know the physical and mental exercises you need to concentrate on to get you to where you need to be.

- You know the extra steps that you need to take to achieve maximum performance. You know that massive gains aren't necessary; and a simple 5% gain in performance can get you noticed, help you get a college scholarship, or get you a major league contract.

- If you have something to offer, you now know what you need to do to get the right people to notice your talents.

Baseball is a truly great sport. It's one of the most difficult games to play and be successful at. If you want to reach the top, you have to do what other players aren't willing to do. Like David Eckstein you have to do the little extras; and as he has proven, you don't need to be 6'4" and 225-lbs. If you have the talent and do the extras that other players don't, you can reach the top of this game.

I can't wait to hear about your success. I know that only a handful of readers will apply all the valuable techniques that have been shared with you in this book. To those readers we know we'll be reading about you in the future.

Some of you may only take an idea or two from this book and run with it. Maybe it helps you make varsity or crack the starting line-up. Maybe it helps you get a college scholarship. If this book helps make you a better ballplayer in any way, then we'll consider the time spent putting it together more than worthwhile.

We wish you success and hope baseball continues to be a big part of your lives. Reach for the peak. You have nothing to lose and everything to gain.

I'd also love to hear from you. Tell me about your successes by writing to me at: *jim@peakpowerbaseball.com.*

Journal Pages

The following is information you should have available at all times:

	Date	Date	Date	Date	Date	Date
60 Yard Dash	___	___	___	___	___	___
Home To First	___	___	___	___	___	___
Bat Speed	___	___	___	___	___	___
Arm Velocity Stalker	___	___	___	___	___	___
Jugs	___	___	___	___	___	___
Height	___					
Weight	___	___	___	___	___	___
PSAT Score	___	___				
SAT Score	___	___	___	___		
ACT Score	___	___	___	___		

	Freshman	Sophomore	Junior	Senior
GPA	___	___	___	___

What am I doing to make myself stronger and faster?

_____

_____

_____

_____

_____

What am I doing to improve my SAT or ACT scores?

_____

_____

_____

_____

_____

What prospective colleges am I interested in?

_____

_____

_____

_____

_____

What is the average SAT or ACT score of each of these schools?

_____

_____

_____

_____

_____

What is the cost of tuition and room and board at these schools?

_____

_____

_____

_____

_____

What is the average academic scholarship at each of these schools based on my GPA and SAT or ACT scores?

_____

_____

_____

_____

_____

What other types of aid can I expect at these schools?

_____

_____

_____

_____

_____

How many baseball scholarships do the schools I'm interested in have available?

_____

_____

_____

_____

_____

Do the schools I am interested in have a need for a player at my position?

_____

_____

_____

_____

_____

Who are the head coaches and recruiting coordinators at each of thse schools - phone numbers - addresses - e-mail addresses?

_____

_____

_____

_____

_____

Am I a Division I, Division II, Division III or a Junior College Player?

_____

_____

Would I rather be a starter at a Division III school or sit the bench at a Division I school?

_____

_____

Am I choosing a school that is right for me academically?

_____

_____

Are there schools that may have a greater need for my skills than the schools I have chosen?

_____

_____

_____

_____

_____

What steps am I taking to make myself more valuable to my coach and team?

_____

_____

_____

_____

_____

Am I working on the mental aspects of my game as well as the physical?

_____

_____

_____

_____

_____

Am I giving 100% to improving myself as a player, or am I only doing enough to get by?

_____

_____

_____

_____

Resource Pages

Athletic Equipment

Baseball Express
Almost everything in baseball - gloves, bats. Great service.
1-800-WE PITCH - send for catalog
www.baseballexpress.com

Hoosier Bat Company
Great 3 piece bat and solid ash bat - reasonable prices.
1-800-228-3787
www.hoosierbat.com

Decker Sports
Overload and under-load bats and balls. Excellent weighted baseball package.
1-800-431-5128
www.deckersports.com

Eastbay
Athletic equipment, shoes, gloves and apparel
1-800-826-2205 - request catalog
www.eastbay.com

The Edge Weighted Glove
Use of this product has been shown to increase velocity 2-3 MPH or more.
1-877-640-4404
www.edge-power.com

Pro Cut
Bat device, hitting system for the proper swing.
1-815-229-2671
www.procut.com

Set-Pro
> Bat speed and arm velocity development equipment program.
> 1-800-890-8803
> www.setpro.com

Nutrition

LifeSource
> Every ballplayer should take a good multi-vitamin daily. This is one of the best. Excellent multi-vitamin. Excellent price. All profits go to Christian organizations.
> www.threadsofgod.com

Netrition
> Great prices and excellent service on most popular nutritional supplements. The Internet's premier nutrition superstore. *(See their ad in this book)*
> www.netrition.com/ppb

Publications

Baseball America
Up-to-date information on professional, college and high school baseball. Articles, statistics and more.
> $51.95 a year
> To subscribe:
>> Baseball America
>> PO Box 2089
>> Durham, NC 27702
>> 1-800-845-2726
> www.baseballamerica.com

Collegiate Baseball

The voice of amateur baseball. Valuable information for coaches and players. College and high school players profiled. Valuable training tips. New product reviews.
$25 for 14 issues
To subscribe:

      Collegiate Baseball Newspaper
      PO Box 50566
      Tucson, AZ 85703

www.baseballnews.com

The Sport Source

The Sport Source gives details on all colleges annually. Programs, number of scholarships, coaches' names, information on the school's baseball program and other sports is available. Over 1000 pages of information.
$35.00 plus shipping - (A great value)
To subscribe:

      1-800-862-3092

www.thesportsource.com

USA Today Baseball Weekly

$39.95 a year
To subscribe:

      1-800-USA-1415

www.baseballweekly.com

Websites

www.baseball-links.com

John Skilton's baseball links to thousands of baseball sites.

www.hsbaseballweb.com

Excellent web-site dealing with all aspects of high school and college baseball. Great interaction on their message boards. Lots of good advice.

www.sportspecific.com/ppb
> Valuable subscription based site. Low annual fee gets an athlete hundreds of pages of training tips and video programs, unlimited e-mail consultation and design of a personal training plan. Very good site.

If you need help with your recruiting efforts, we have numerous ways to help you.

Visit our Web Site at www.peakpowerbaseball.com

or call us toll-free at 888-895-2961